"Warm and accessible, yet profound and insightful. Chokyi Nyima Rinpoche offers compelling advice for our times. This book is a treasure of timeless wisdom that today is needed more than ever."

—Cher

"My friend and teacher Chokyi Nyima Rinpoche is a seasoned and authentic Dzogchen master. He has written a book that throws a lifeline to all of us struggling in the sea of ignorance, desire, and hatred. As he says, 'Dharma is not a hobby,' but it is a very serious business indeed. Dharma can save us from the ocean of forgetfulness so that we may remember who we really are: beings of light, love, and wisdom. Complete liberation is possible if we do the work and guaranteed if we follow our teacher's advice. Rinpoche takes us through the stages of Buddhist practice leading to the joy and freedom of the Great Perfection, Dzogchen. Rinpoche emphasizes the necessity of embracing the truths of impermanence and dependent origination as the sources of our future enlightenment. This is a truly inspiring book for all practitioners."

—Richard Gere

"Here we learn how to truly appreciate all of life—in full sadness and full happiness—with the simple recipe of being calm, kind, and aware, and full of joy in everything."

—Piet Hut, professor of astrophysics and
head of the program in Interdisciplinary Studies,
Institute for Adv‌

"Different traditions differ in how they understand and use the term *mindfulness*, yet they agree on the nondual nature of mind and the need for authentic instruction and practice. As venerable Chokyi Nyima Rinpoche describes in this elegant, succinct, and extremely useful primer on essential Dharma as a way of being, there are many different methods in the universe of meditation, but in the end—and from the beginning—those that are authentic and trustworthy serve one purpose, and that is realized, embodied wakefulness."

—Jon Kabat-Zinn, author of *Full Catastrophe Living* and *Meditation Is Not What You Think*

Sadness
Love
Openness

THE BUDDHIST PATH OF JOY

Chokyi Nyima Rinpoche

Shambhala
Boulder 2018

Shambhala Publications, Inc.
4720 Walnut Street
Boulder, Colorado 80301
www.shambhala.com

9 8 7 6 5 4 3 2 1

First Edition

Printed in the United States of America

♾ This edition is printed on acid-free paper that meets the American
National Standards Institute Z39.48 Standard.
♻ This book is printed on 30% postconsumer recycled paper. For more
information please visit www.shambhala.com.

Distributed in the United States by Penguin Random House LLC and in
Canada by Random House of Canada Ltd

LIBRARY OF CONGRESS CATALOGING-IN-PUBLICATION DATA
Names: Chökyi Nyima, Rinpoche, 1951– author.
Title: Sadness, love, openness: the Buddhist path of joy / Chökyi Nyima
Rinpoche.
Description: First edition. | Boulder: Shambhala, 2018.
Identifiers: LCCN 2017045774 | ISBN 9781611804881 (pbk.: alk. paper)
Subjects: LCSH: Religious life—Buddhism. | Spiritual life—Buddhism.
Classification: LCC BQ7775 .C53 2018 | DDC 294.3/444—dc23
LC record available at https://lccn.loc.gov/2017045774

Deep sadness, because nothing lasts.

Fervent love, because all beings are my beloved family.

Lucid openness, because this ordinary mind is full awakening.

Sheer joy, because all of this is true.

CONTENTS

INTRODUCTION

In Buddhism, gaining concrete, firsthand experience with the instructions is paramount. If we are searching for freedom and awakening, treating topics such as impermanence and suffering, love and compassion, or insight into the nature of the mind as abstract concepts is not sufficient. The only way to truly understand these crucial points is through direct experience. Only then will the Dharma be applicable and truly effective.

What are the experiences that the teachings of the Buddha are founded on? They are sadness, love, and openness. Although they appear to be quite different, sadness and openness are in fact intimately connected. The profound sadness that overwhelms us when we understand the impermanent nature of all phenomena opens us up to the world around us. We open our hearts and begin to notice our fellow beings. We see how we all must face the hardships of life; we understand the fleeting nature of our joys; and we become aware of how much worry, pain, and suffering we all go through in our lives. In this way, we realize that we all share similar painful experiences. Knowing what others go through and feel, we cannot help but sympathize with them, and the wish to help and protect our fellow beings naturally wells up in us. This wish to help and protect arises from love, and the more we open our eyes to others' suffering and delusion, the stronger our love becomes. Love clears the mind of the thick fog of desire, anger, and ignorance. Love is like the sun that burns through the fog, dissolving it, until only vast openness and clarity remain. When nothing but boundless openness and lucidity remain, we come face-to-face with the basic nature of all phenomena beyond concepts.

Still, as thoughts reemerge, the fog inevitably reappears. But now we know—from our own experience—that freedom and awakening are always right here, within us. This realization gives rise to an indescribable joy. We have experienced for ourselves that awakening is a genuine option, for us and for everyone else—how wonderful! The heartfelt wish that everyone may awaken to true freedom is born in us and consumes us to the point where our attachment and delusion seem to dissolve naturally. All the while, we see the world for what it is, utterly impermanent and painful, and our sadness grows ever more profound. Yet our sadness is now accompanied by genuine love and affection and a deep sense of responsibility brought on by the certainty that if we simply stay on course, we will be able to make a true and lasting difference everywhere we go. This is how sadness, love, and openness sustain Dharma practitioners.

Sadness

SETTING OUT

We all know the importance of having the proper attitude when we begin a new project. This book is about the Dharma—the teachings of the Buddha—and when working with the Dharma, it's important to be motivated by a particular wish. It is important to feel that, as we learn and train, we want the outcome to be useful and beneficial for everyone—for all beings. Therefore, at this point it would be good to think like this:

> *What I am about to do now is something that has the power to overcome all my negative emotions and confused thoughts. It will lead me along a path that leads from one joyful moment to another, the direct way to liberation and awakening. I want to share that joy with all beings.*

Thinking like this changes us right away. It calms us down and relaxes us. It makes us open up to others, and we begin to notice the sadness and pain that everyone carries with them. Such a mind that truly cares about the well-being and happiness of others is a beautiful garden where flowers of wisdom and insight can bloom.

WHAT WE LIVE FOR

Buddhism views this life as just one among many. This current life began when we were born, and it will end when one day we die. During this life, we rely on certain things to keep us from harm and to support us. As small children, we rely on our parents for safety and comfort. As we grow up, we go to school and receive an education, trusting that this will be good for us. When at some point we feel we have learned enough, we look for a job that can pay our bills and afford us entertainment and fun. We rely on all these things—along with our family, friends, possessions, and social standing—to give structure to our lives and make us happy. Actually, everything we do is motivated by the search for happiness

NOTHING LASTS

As we look for happiness, however, we often find that our situation ends up quite different from what we actually wanted. The reason we end up with that experience is that everything in this world occurs due to something else. In other words, nothing exists independently. Buddhism refers to this as conditioned existence, and conditioned existence is characterized by being impermanent. We may be very intelligent people who have accomplished a lot, or maybe we're just lucky and everything is naturally going our way. In any case, nothing stays the same, and sooner or later the winds of fortune shift. Suddenly we find ourselves in a radically different situation. Throughout it all, we keep getting older, and one day we will die and be no more. This may sound a bit harsh, but it's a simple fact of life. And if we are willing to face facts, we are already opening up to something that is much greater than our usual concerns.

THE MEANING OF LIFE

We wish so much for our lives to be meaningful. And many of us think that a meaningful life is something we can work toward, through certain events that we can experience, things we can acquire, or people we can meet. But what are we really looking for? What is actually achievable in this life? What do we get out of all the things we do? When this life is over, we can't take anything with us. Forget about money and possessions—we can't even bring the people we love the most. This life culminates in a forced and final separation from everything and everyone we have ever loved and held dear. We have pushed ourselves so hard to get something out of this life. We have been swimming in a sea of thoughts and ideas. And maybe we have achieved a lot. Maybe we have money in the bank. Perhaps we are popular and have plenty of friends and a loving family. But whatever we might have, we will have to bid it all farewell on the day death comes knocking on our door.

Think carefully: Have you achieved everything you wanted? Is everything just the way it should be? If the answer is yes, then all is fine and well. But very few people are perfectly happy and content with their lives. To use a Tibetan expression, such people are as rare as stars in the daytime sky. Let's be honest: we all know the nagging feeling that something is missing, that things aren't as good as they should be—the feeling that our life should be better.

THOUGHTS AND EMOTIONS

The way our minds work makes it quite impossible to be content. We are controlled by our thoughts, which are restless. They are always fluctuating, never capable of resting in calmness, joy, and contentment, which are simply not in the nature of thoughts. There's always a nagging feeling that something is not good enough, a voice whispering to us that everything would be much better, if only. . .

Thinking automatically creates a perception of things as not being quite right. We are never truly at ease, because we remain incapable of appreciating the present moment just as it is. There's always something we wish for and something else we want to avoid. We keep shifting between hope and fear, which in turn create other emotions—emotions that can grow strong and destructive. Take attachment and aversion, for instance. When attachment and aversion begin to shape our consciousness, it is only a matter of time before they will drive us to act. Sooner or later we will go for what we desire and try to avoid what we dislike. In fact, anything we think, say, or do is the expression of the emotions that roam about our consciousness. And such actions have consequences. When our minds are confused by thoughts and drunk on emotions, the results of our actions are going to be painful for ourselves and others. There's no other possible outcome.

THE NATURE OF THOUGHTS

This may sound strange, but even though our thoughts manifest in such negative ways and have such severe results, the true nature of thoughts is actually nothing but wisdom. Thoughts do not contain anything but wakefulness. That's what we need to realize. The Dharma is here to help us discover that the true nature of thoughts is nothing but wakefulness. This is the only way we can break through the deceptions of thought.

In the end, this is the real reason that we receive instruction and try to comprehend what the Dharma is about. This is why we put the teachings into practice; this is why we meditate. If we allow our thoughts to keep acting as they do now, we will never find happiness in the present moment. We will always be running away from one thing and chasing another.

DHARMA PRACTICE IS NOT A HOBBY

The Dharma warns us against the destructive power of our thoughts and teaches us how to recognize their true nature. It reveals what a thought actually is—wisdom and wakefulness. The Dharma invites us to discover the wisdom, compassion, and power that are intrinsic to our thinking. That's the purpose of Dharma practice—to enable us to recognize and familiarize ourselves with the true nature of thoughts. Eventually, we can become perfectly free and confident in our recognition. Therefore, it is important to realize that the Dharma is no hobby. It is crucial that we understand the purpose of the Dharma and know how to practice it correctly. The Dharma must become a real priority in our lives in order to truly cultivate this recognition.

WORRIES

As things stand, nothing in this world makes any real sense or has any deeper meaning. Fame, status, power, money—however much we may have, it's all unsatisfying and fragile. We work so hard to get what we want, but when we finally achieve what we wish for, it's suddenly no longer all that exciting. We quickly feel bored and lose interest. Still, we lose sleep worrying about how to protect our investments while fantasizing about future achievements. The worries of those who have little to no possessions are usually limited to finding food and having a roof over their heads. Don't get me wrong—I'm not saying that poverty makes people content. I am saying that the more we rely on external circumstances to make us happy, the more miserable we become.

What good is material abundance if we are mentally impoverished? We need to feel happy, secure, prosperous, and at ease, but aren't those all primarily *mental* needs? True happiness comes from appreciating whatever we have and being less worried, less scared. Yet we're always on the lookout for something. That's the way it was when we were children, and we're still like that today. What is it we are really looking for? It's the feeling of success. But what does that even mean? And how do we get there? While we keep hoping, trying, working, and toiling, we also keep growing older, and one day our health begins to fail. The tragedy is that we never reach a point where we feel that we got what we wanted.

KARMA

Why would we need the Dharma? Why is it a good idea to study the teachings of the Buddha? Studying the Dharma is a good idea because we don't see things clearly, the way they really are. Hour after hour, day after day, month after month, and year after year, we are constantly fooled by illusions. Nothing is the way it seems. Nothing lasts. Yet our experience nevertheless feels so real, and so we react with attachment, aversion, or indifference.

Karma is action—actions that we take that leave an imprint on us that determine our future experience. Whenever we like or sympathize with something or someone, this is a subtle form of negative karma. That's because liking something is a subtle aspect of attachment. And whenever we dislike or disagree with someone or something, this is a subtle form of negative karma. That's because not liking something is a form of aversion. The same goes for indifference: "I don't care" is basically an expression of ignorance, so it too is a subtle form of negative karma. If we check, it's easy to notice that our thoughts always take one of those three tracks.

In short, things that actually aren't real attract us. But because we experience them as real, we also instinctively assume that they are here to stay. That's how our delusion works. The same applies to the things we don't like. Whenever we encounter someone or something we don't like, it feels so solid and real. Our feelings are intrusive and convincing, and so we never stop to consider whether our experience even reflects the way things actually are.

UNDERSTANDING BUDDHISM

People of other faiths are often quite knowledgeable about their religion, but sadly that's not always the case with Buddhists. To be honest, the majority of Buddhists don't know what Buddhism is really about, that is, what it all comes down to. Many people get caught up in ritual or philosophical details that are part of the whole enterprise, of course, but aren't in any way crucial to the heart of the tradition. In that way, Buddhism comes to appear very much like any other typical religion. Indeed, on the surface, what we do is not that different from people who follow other religions. We try to be nice and caring and good, and we may tell ourselves that this is basically what Buddhism is about. We believe in the Buddha, while others believe in God, Allah, or some other divinity, but basically it all amounts to the same thing. Actually, there are quite a few Buddhists who think like that!

However, as modern and intelligent Buddhists of the twenty-first century, it is our responsibility to be fully aware of what Buddhism is really about. Why do we practice the Buddha's teachings? How do we practice them in the best, most effective way? And what is the net result? Very few people actually know the answers to these questions. Obviously, the way we behave is not unimportant. But for all Buddhist schools the key issue has always been the understanding of two topics: the two truths and dependent origination.

The two truths refer to ultimate truth and relative truth. The ultimate is the nature of reality, the way things actually are, while the relative is the way things appear to us, the way they seem to be.

Dependent origination means that everything comes into being in dependence on something else. In other words, all existence is conditioned and contingent. Dependent origination is deep and complex. It's rare to meet people who truly understand it. Nonetheless, dependent origination lies at the very heart of the teachings of the Buddha.

A famous Buddhist verse states:

> All phenomena appear from causes.
> The Buddha has taught those causes,
> And also that which brings about their cessation.
> This is what the Great Mendicant has taught.

So, as modern, intelligent Buddhists, it should be our goal to understand dependent origination.

WHY BOTHER?

Before we do anything else, we need to be clear about why we follow the teachings of the Buddha at all. We need to understand and experience for ourselves what Buddhism is really about, and we need to know what results we gain from our practice.

The reason we study the teachings of the Buddha is that our perception is out of touch with reality, and our emotions cause pain for others and ourselves. And so we study the teachings of the Buddha because we want to stop being deluded. This is why we listen, reflect, and seek to gain practical experience with the Dharma. The result is ultimate awakening—realizing the true nature of our thoughts, those very thoughts that otherwise chase us around, preventing us from seeing things the way they actually are. In their basic nature, our thoughts are wisdom—pure, nonconceptual wisdom. When we study and train in applying the teachings of the Buddha, it is for the purpose of directly experiencing this realization.

VARIATIONS

All Buddhist schools agree that dependent origination is the pivotal point. In fact, if we have fully understood dependent origination, there isn't really anything left for us to understand. Everyone agrees on this. Still, the different schools explain dependent origination slightly differently. That is because people aren't all the same. The different traditions teach in their own specific ways so that everyone may find a means of understanding—it may be pithy and concise or complex and elaborate. While presentations and styles may differ in this way, the topic always remains the same—the way things appear through dependent origination, and the true nature of that which appears.

PRACTICE IS A MUST

Unless we practice the teachings through study, reflection, and meditation, we are stuck in the rut of being controlled by our thoughts and habits. The way we think of and perceive the world is mistaken. Our consciousness is structured such that no matter how carefully we may think, no matter how hard we may try to grasp the world around us, the conclusion we arrive at is always different from what things are actually like, and it is our acting upon this mistaken perception that leads to suffering.

THINKING, EMOTION, AND ACTION

Our uncontrolled thoughts prevent us from feeling content and at ease in the present moment. We constantly get the sense that there is something else to do and achieve, something other than what is here right now. There's always something we want to go for and something else we're trying to avoid. Pressure builds, and once we give in, we behave in ways that are regrettable, both for others and for ourselves. Whether subtle or crude, our greed and anger keep spawning new feelings and thoughts, and so matters keep complicating. For example, we might begin to think of ourselves as very special and so develop an unhealthy type of pride. That conceit and self-cherishing can fill us with jealousy and envy, making us unable to feel happy when things go well for others. Such a frame of mind is unwholesome now and destructive in the long run.

ATTACHMENT, AVERSION, AND IGNORANCE

Our thoughts, feelings, and ideas about the world are all cogs in the machinery that make up our thinking mind. Even when we just simply *like* something, we are already busy building up desire. On the other hand, whenever there is something we dislike, we are already involved with a subtle form of aversion. Finally, whenever we don't care and just don't want to bother, we are feeding our dullness and ignorance. In the end, no matter how we think and what we may think of, there are only those three options: liking, disliking, and not wanting to bother. We should also remember that the ultimate source of both attachment and aversion is ignorance. All of them feed our deluded consciousness, so we can be certain that the future will bring even more confusion and that our negative emotions will become more overwhelming than they are now.

Attachment, aversion, and ignorance make suffering a sure thing. The more negative emotions we develop based on these, the more miserable our experience of the world will be. Buddhist cosmology speaks of infernal realms where the manifestation of suffering is excruciating and completely overwhelming. On the other hand, it is said that if we keep generating positive thoughts, we will sooner or later experience realms with divine pleasures. Yet none of those states endures—they all are temporary. Like everything else produced by causes and conditions, heavenly states are impermanent. As long as our actions and thoughts depend on attachment, aversion, and ignorance, we are bound to suffer.

THE OPTIMAL POINT OF DEPARTURE

Our task as Buddhists is to break free from the circle of life that involves ignorance and suffering. The good news is that our current situation as humans offers a unique opportunity to do just that. How? Buddhist cosmology describes three types of existence, also known as realms: the desire realm, the form realm, and the formless realm. As humans we are born in the desire realm, and here we will automatically experience much suffering and crude negative emotions. That is not the case with those who are born in a divine abode in the form realm or the formless realm. But no matter how gorgeous and delightful the higher, divine states may seem, the ideal realm for profound and effective practice is that of humans.

Our human body is subject to the influence of the elements, and our consciousness experiences all sorts of negative emotions. However, if we receive powerful instructions on the way to actualize wisdom, we will soon be able to manifest a wide range of the wonderful qualities of awakening. In a divine state, such a thing doesn't happen. The body and mind of a god may seem far more splendid and magnificent, but in terms of awakening from ignorance, they are not ideal. That's why we really could not be in a more fortunate situation than this. As humans in this world, we have everything it takes. But still, we have to seize the opportunity and accept the challenge. Otherwise, we'll just stagger along in confusion and misery. And when one day this life is over, we'll proceed to even more ignorance and suffering. In short, our future well-being hinges on our learning to apply the instructions.

HOPE AND FEAR

Why do we suffer? We suffer because of hope and fear. Wherever there is hope and fear, suffering follows automatically. When we are unable to appreciate what we have here and now, we keep hoping for something else. At the same time, we fear the unknown. We suffer because nothing is certain. We can never know for sure what is going to happen next. We don't even know what will happen five minutes from now.

A LACK OF LOVE

We live in a time when many teenagers are depressed and feel their lives are empty and meaningless. Some even go so far as to take their own lives. Others numb their pain with drugs and alcohol. The problem is not that they lack education or resources, but they are nevertheless deeply unhappy. Other kids act out their feelings by becoming cold and uncaring. Here modern technology definitely carries part of the blame. Technology is useful, but it can also do much harm, as when computer games turn violence into entertainment. In any case, at the root of all this is confusion. And where does this confusion come from? It comes from a lack of love.

SHALLOWNESS

We must take care not to become shallow people. Religion can easily turn into a sort of entertainment, a way to socialize and make new friends. Some cozy feeling of community mixed with a dash of faith, a ritual here and there, and some nice tunes to sing along the way—if that's our approach to religion, then whatever we do is going to be rather superficial, and we will lose any real sense of what our religion is about. This sort of thing also happens in Buddhist circles. Of course, that doesn't mean we should just forget about our temples, texts, images, special garments, rosaries, and the like. But it is important to remember that all those things are secondary.

BE AWARE

Being aware from moment to moment is key. That will give us so much opportunity. Buddhism has a lot of techniques, it is vast and logical, and its wisdom is razor sharp. We're getting everything we could possibly ask for, and then some! In fact, we may be somewhat spoiled. Because sadly, the practice and the practitioner often remain separate. And that's not how it's supposed to be—the practice and the practitioner should click and become one! Genuine practice is not rigid or fanatical. Genuine practice means being aware from moment to moment. The goal is to become calmer, kinder, more accommodating, more at ease, and more intelligent. It's all very logical.

STUCK ON THE SURFACE

When we remember what Buddhism is fundamentally about, we will also become serious about our practice. We need to know the purpose and the importance of the things we do. Otherwise it's easy to get caught up in a lot of details that actually aren't important at all. Genuine practice is not just thinking that Buddhism is interesting, or reading books and listening to talks to acquire new knowledge. Genuine practice is not about exotic, colorful rituals either. Genuine practice is not a matter of knowing the right way to prepare a Buddhist shrine, it's not a matter of dress, and it's not a matter knowing what to say or how to behave.

But it's easy to get caught up in all those things; it's easy to miss the sense of what really matters. Don't get me wrong— I'm not saying that it's bad if we know how to prepare a shrine; indeed, it's a very good thing to know. But it's important that we don't get too caught up in the details and stuck on the surface of things. Our practice is authentic when we have a clear sense of the crucial points and never forget them.

A BALANCING ACT

Figuring out the way to practice isn't difficult at all. When we listen to a talk or read a text and then give some thought to what we learn, it's all very clear and logical. If we are genuinely interested, it isn't hard to understand. The difficult part is taking to heart what we learn. But that's not because the instructions themselves are very demanding. We won't be subjected to a lot of hardships and trials. Instead, Buddhism is about achieving balance. The Buddha kept emphasizing that we need to find a good balance between rigid austerity and our thirst for enjoyments and satisfaction. It's about finding a balance between these two extremes. That's all there is to it.

GROWING UP

Why is it so difficult for us to apply the teachings? Something must be holding us back, preventing us from making progress. Let's imagine that this "something" is an especially profound and impenetrable obstacle. In that case, our lack of progress could be conveniently excused. But really, there's nothing very profound about what's holding us back. Our minds are immature and childish—that's all. We are not mature, so our experiences keep deceiving us. The good news is that as soon as we realize that we are immature, we no longer are. We won't be fooled anymore.

TWO PATHS

For many people, studying and reflecting are the two main ways to a deeper understanding of the Buddhist view. One may read Buddhist books, attend public seminars and teachings on Buddhist thought, and reflect on the truths that they convey. But there is also a third approach, another path, that goes a step further. Here, one forms a personal relationship with an experienced and realized teacher who knows the student well and who is aware of what level he or she is at. Such a teacher can then in a timely manner provide his or her students with the right kind of instruction and guide them all the way to awakening, step-by-step. Knowing such a master, and maintaining a close relationship with him or her, is a rare and extremely fortunate situation.

These days it can be difficult for people to arrange their lives so that they can stay near a teacher of that kind. But the fact remains that while studying and reflecting are excellent, they are not enough. We need actual firsthand experience with what the teachings talk about. Nowadays, masters are offering online courses that allow everyone to receive authentic and effective guidance in meditation practice. Studying and reflecting are excellent, but they are not enough. We need actual firsthand experience through meditation.

MERIT

Why don't more people take the opportunity to follow a program that combines study and practical training? The reason is that something is required. That requirement is merit, which is the result of positive actions done in the past. For example, we possess merit if in a previous life we formed a sincere wish to study the teachings of the Buddha. Apart from that, encountering the Dharma doesn't simply happen by coincidence or a stroke of luck. That's not how it works. Things won't happen before we are ready. It takes a lot of merit and fortunate circumstances.

The message is as clear as day, and once we start practicing, we quickly notice the results. Why then isn't Buddhism more popular? Why aren't there more people who practice? We humans are intelligent, and we value education and the ability to think clearly and logically. We also have all sorts of aids and appliances to help us along the way. In that light, one would expect everyone to be busy learning about the Dharma and how to apply the instructions. But things just don't work that way. Discovering and benefiting from the teachings of the Buddha is the culmination of a process of mental development that has evolved over countless lifetimes. In Buddhism, we call this process *accumulating merit*.

RELIGION AND MATERIALISM

Why do we suffer? We suffer because of fear—fear and doubt. For protection, we then turn to education, money, and religion. Before, people depended on a religion to give meaning and direction in their lives. These days, people often rely on a materialist worldview—the view that reality comes down to matter—to give them clarity and guidance. Whether the framework we rely on is religious or materialist, the basic sense of dependency is the same. We feel that there is something, beyond us, that everything ultimately stands and falls with.

DELUSION

It's crucial that we understand why Dharma is important and why practice is necessary. Without the Dharma, we are fooled by our thoughts and experiences. Without the Dharma, we will never be able to look beyond the surface of things. Without the Dharma, our outlook—the way we perceive the world and its inhabitants, as well as ourselves and our feelings—remains superficial. Our suffering, our happiness, and all the other experiences we may have—none of it has any basis in reality, but the truth of this escapes us because we are ignorant of the impermanent and dependent nature of all phenomena. In short, there is a fundamental discrepancy between our perception of reality and the way things actually are. We suffer from delusions about everything. We sleepwalk through life, clueless about what's going on around us and where we are heading. The purpose of the Dharma is to enable us to break free from such a way of life through the cultivation of wisdom.

TWO KINDS OF KNOWLEDGE

One of the many meanings of the word *dharma* is "phenomenon," meaning something that can be experienced. In other words, when we want to study the Dharma, we have a wish to learn about all that can be experienced, in terms of both the way things appear to us and the way they actually are. Knowing how things really are is obviously the most important. If we are only aware of the way things seem to be, we will never understand what is actually the case. That sort of understanding will always be superficial. In short, if insight and wisdom are to unfold, we have to take into account both the way things appear and how they are in reality.

In this context, Buddhism introduces many concepts and categories concerning the way we sentient beings are built and how we function. We learn about the different elements that constitute our body and consciousness, the nature of our experiences, what it means for something to exist, how things occur in dependence on causes and conditions, and so on. Many of these topics are straightforward and not that hard to understand.

EVERYTHING IS POSSIBLE

Certain topics in Buddhism, however, are not within the reach of our immediate experience or capacity for rational inquiry. They are matters that only an awakened mind—a buddha mind—can fully comprehend. A good example is karmic cause and effect. Which actions produce which results? Nevertheless, in the context of karma, we can still draw on our own experience. If we think of our own experiences of sadness and joy, happiness and suffering, there doesn't seem to be any limit to how good or how awful things can get.

We can also see that none of our perceptions last. Everything keeps changing. What exists in one moment may no longer be there in the next, and consequently the situation has changed completely. We can learn a lot from paying attention to our experience. It's not hard to see that it must be possible to experience the world in ways that are radically different from our present experience. For example, in a god-like state, one perceives everything as heavenly beauty and bliss, while others may be trapped in a hellish state of pain and suffering. Our minds have the potential for all sorts of experiences. In short, the subtler teachings of Buddhism can be approached through relying on a combination of scripture and investigation of our own experience.

HOW DO WE SEE THE WORLD?

We experience the world around us as real and lasting. The things we perceive out there appear to really be there, seemingly enduring through time. But the world actually is not as it appears. Nothing lasts for more than an instant. Everything changes from moment to moment, and yet we still think that our perceptions are real and genuine. The more we get stuck in that way of thinking, the stronger our negative emotions will grow. And the more those emotions take charge, the harder and more painful life becomes.

In other words, our problems arise because we perceive the world and beings as enduring and independent. That's a distorted perspective, and it tricks us. How then can we change our perspective? How can we move on? We may work hard at improving our thoughts and emotions, but as long as the framework for that is a consciousness that is fundamentally deluded, we won't find any lasting solution to our troubles.

WHAT CAN HELP US?

We need a radical solution—something that can cut through our experience of a real and lasting world. The problem is ignorance, which manifests as our continuous distinction between self and other, and our belief that both are solid, lasting, and real, and this ignorance resides within us. That's why we need to find the solution within ourselves. The dualistic split in consciousness, which creates all the trouble, can be cured only by its complete opposite.

The remedy therefore is nondual awareness, which is actually already present within us right now, in this very moment, even though we fail to see it. We don't realize what we already have. Please understand this: the root of all our problems is within ourselves, but so is the perfect solution. It's our minds that create our delusions and negative emotions. And the solution, the antidote—that which is utterly beyond delusion, negative emotions, suffering, and all dualistic constructs—is also present in our own mind right now. And that's what Buddhism is really about: solving the problem by realizing the solution within. There are lots of things we can do to reach that point. For example, we can train to become better at giving and sharing.

GIVING AND SHARING

Whenever we don't feel like sharing with others, we are narrowing the scope of our minds. Stinginess makes us feel tense and unnatural. It's painful to be that way; our lives become rigid. On the other hand, whenever we are able to share with others or give something away, this immediately frees the mind. It's almost like magic. Sharing and giving create an immediate sense of spaciousness, joy, and freedom. In fact, the mere intention to share is as powerful as the act itself.

There is a meditation practice known as *giving and taking*. In this meditation, we mentally give away all our most cherished possessions and accomplishments, offering them to all beings. At the same time, we take upon ourselves all their problems—all their sadness, confusion, and suffering. This is a very powerful practice. If we engage in it sincerely and with an open mind, we naturally develop all the wonderful qualities that come with being generous. Training in that kind of exchange will enable us to realize the nature of reality and the wisdom that lies at the core of our being.

On the other hand, the less we're able to share and to give, the harder it is to realize the nature of all phenomena, and the more painful living becomes. But as our stinginess wanes, we become more flexible and carefree. Life becomes easier and we find ourselves less confused. Quite naturally, our minds brighten. It all comes down to applying the right methods. Skillful use of the right methods yields tangible results. And generosity is just such a method.

LETTING GO

Another powerful method is to cut the ties that usually bind us. Whenever you feel there's something you absolutely must get your hands on, or something you couldn't possibly bear to lose, just try letting it go. Release it instead of holding on. Letting go is wholesome and healing. Instead of hanging on to all sorts of ideas about what it takes to be happy, just let go. Be generous. Try to let go, right now, in this very moment. The benefits reveal themselves immediately.

As soon as we let go of the things we hanker after and set them free, without holding on to anything, we experience freedom and joy that are unmediated and real.

IMPERMANENCE TEACHES US TO LET GO

The ability to let go comes naturally when we begin to challenge our perception of the world as real and lasting. The world is impermanent. One day everything we know will be gone. That's simply how it is. Everything ends and ceases to be. Deep down, we know this already; we just don't like to think about it. But in fact, everything changes from one moment to the next. All the things we name and label, the things we like or dislike, don't actually exist as something unchanging and independent of circumstances. When we take a closer look, we find that none of the things we take to be real actually exist.

If we think well and apply reason, this is something we can figure out quite quickly. But our intellectual understanding must turn into actual experience. Otherwise, even though we understand intellectually that everything is unreal, we continue to feel that things are real and solid. Instead, we need to recognize that these perceptions are just that—perceptions—and they don't reflect the way things actually are.

WHEN THINKING MAKES SENSE

We have to start thinking in a more meaningful way. Then we'll automatically move in the right direction. Meaningful thinking means taking to heart that nothing lasts and nothing is as we perceive. And it means reminding ourselves, again and again, that this is how it is. We can make great progress doing this. By coming to understand the impermanent and illusory nature of everything, we slowly but surely set ourselves free—even if our understanding is actually the product of conceptions and therefore not yet born out of direct, personal experience.

What does it mean to become *free*? In this context, it means that we gradually weaken the power our emotions have over us. When we're no longer so rigidly controlled by our emotions, we no longer experience the same degree of despair and misery when things don't work out as planned. In short, thinking and reflecting in meaningful ways produces many substantial results.

THE THREEFOLD PERSPECTIVE

The vajra vehicle, as the tantric Buddhist teachings are called, speaks of a threefold perspective, which is a particular view of the world. In this context, we cultivate an attitude that transforms our ordinary perceptions into enlightened or divine expressions. All visual appearances are regarded as pure, everything we hear is the sound of mantra or divine sound, and all of our thoughts and emotions are perceived as expressions of wisdom. That's how one is supposed to go through life as a practitioner of the vajra vehicle.

This can be a difficult attitude to maintain, so there is also a simpler alternative, which is to remember impermanence and the illusory nature of all things. No matter what we experience, we must recall that it is all impermanent and unreal. Whenever we bring to mind impermanence and the illusory nature of all phenomena, we're following in the footsteps of the Buddha. Then we're on the right track. We need to open up and become aware of all the good qualities that we already possess.

STUDYING

The great Indian master Nagarjuna said that Buddhist teachings are always based on two kinds of truth: the relative and the ultimate. If no one had ever told us that there are two types of truth, we would probably never think that life could be more than the way it appears. That shows how important it is to study the words of the Buddha and reflect on their meaning. But studying and reflecting is not enough—we need to arrive at a direct and personal experience.

EXPERIENCE

It is with experience that meditation becomes important, because only through direct experience can liberation become an actual possibility, and meditation is the gateway to experience. Therefore, Buddhist practice has three aspects: studying, reflecting, and meditating.

Meditation can take many forms. If our goal is to understand the relative and the ultimate truths, then our practice certainly doesn't have to be confined to our meditation cushion. There are many different methods available to us. The methods differ widely, and the results also tend to differ significantly from person to person.

MEDITATING WHILE THINKING

There is, however, one particular method that benefits everyone alike: acknowledging that nothing lasts. We instinctively feel that things are going to stay more or less the same and that the people around us will remain, but that's not the case. If we can, we should try our best to understand that things really aren't the way they seem at all. But if that seems a bit far off at first, it's still very good to give some thought to the impermanence of things. Even if we just take a quick look around, it's easy to prove the truth of impermanence. So, first we must acknowledge that things don't last. Then we need to bring that understanding to mind again and again, until we deeply understand that everything is impermanent and transient. That is a genuine Buddhist meditation.

These days, a lot of people associate meditation with sitting on a cushion, feeling calm and relaxed. So perhaps it sounds a bit strange that reflecting on impermanence can be a meditation. But across all Buddhist traditions, observing the impermanent nature of all phenomena is an important contemplative practice.

THE IMPACT

What happens when we reflect on the impermanent nature of all things? What happens when we really take to heart the fact that everything we are fond of, everything we consider important and meaningful, is going to be lost? What happens when we understand that no matter how well we take care of ourselves, one another, or the whole world for that matter, it's just a question of time before we will have to say goodbye to it all? When we clearly understand that that's how life is, when we actually *get* that, then we will find ourselves overwhelmed by a deep sadness, a sorrow more heartbreaking than anything we have ever known, but this impact is necessary.

THE GIFT OF SADNESS

Reflecting on impermanence is not meant to make us miserable. But without that sorrow of knowing nothing will last, we will never get anywhere on our path. Sadness makes it possible for us to gain something that is much more precious than anything we could imagine. That is why we must contemplate impermanence. If there were nothing to gain, it would be foolish to think about these things—we would just be making ourselves miserable for no reason. But there's a deep meaning to it all. When it dawns on us what the world is actually like, and we are consequently struck by overwhelming sadness, the next step comes naturally. We draw the logical conclusion that all things are impermanent and begin training in letting go.

BECOMING REALISTIC

Gradually, we are able to let go of all the things we used to chase after blindly, all the things that used to bind us and control us. We develop that ability through a discernment that we normally don't possess. Instinctively, we begin to let go, because *now we know*. Whether we like it or not, sooner or later we will be forced to let everything go, so when we know this, it makes perfect sense to lessen our clinging now. Unless we take impermanence into account, we will just continue holding on to things, which in the end will only bring us pain and deprive our lives of meaning. On the other hand, if we have really understood that nothing lasts and that everything is unreal and illusory, then letting go is easy. Actually, it happens by itself without effort. Reflecting on the impermanent and illusory nature of all things is a very powerful practice.

FRESH EYES

Understanding impermanence is no magical feat, but it dramatically, almost magically, changes our experience of the world. It makes us capable of actions that used to be impossible. We begin to look at our world and ourselves from a completely new perspective, and that profound shift in outlook is actually at the heart of all Dharma practice. In fact, we can measure our spiritual progress by how often we remember that all conditioned phenomena are impermanent. For the most accomplished practitioners, this happens quite spontaneously. They have already then let go.

WAKING UP

We begin to awaken, thinking: *I'm fooling myself. The way I experience the world and those around me, the way I experience my emotions and myself—it's all wrong, and it's painful. All the stuff that I worry about—the things I must have, the things I cannot bear to lose, and the things I try to avoid—it all just keeps me trapped. When I see things in that confused way, it has nothing to do with how they actually are. Moreover, since I am doing this to myself, I am only causing my own suffering. How sad and meaningless!*

BREAKING FREE

We then commit ourselves to breaking free of this outlook: *I'm done! From now on, I want to see things for what they really are.*

I won't be a slave to my own delusions anymore. I know my perception of the world is completely out of touch with reality. All my daydreams and fantasies, all my worries and fears—they are all trivial and pointless!

As we think in this way, our wish to be free grows stronger. The power of that wish then transforms into a key that unlocks Buddhism's vast treasury of methods and instructions.

OPENING UP

When we realize that everything is impermanent and unreal, we open up to the pain and suffering of others. That is how love and compassion become heartfelt and genuine. No matter how many praises we sing of love and compassion, such qualities won't awaken and flourish unless we acknowledge impermanence.

FROM SADNESS TO STRENGTH

So many wonderful qualities are already present within us, just waiting to be discovered. The key lies in understanding that things are impermanent and unreal. Sadness, of course, is not an end in itself. But deep sorrow comes with realizing that everything we previously took to be lasting and real is actually just about to disappear—and it never even existed in the first place. Such sadness and disillusionment have a wonderful effect. Sorrow makes us let go. As we stop chasing futile and ultimately painful goals, we embark on the spiritual path with superior strength and resolve.

THE HEALING POWER OF THE DHARMA

Listening to the Dharma changes us. We begin to feel a profound joy, but we are also struck by tremendous sadness at our confusion and the uncertainty of our situation. So our hearts are heavy, but at the same time we feel that we need not despair, because we have at long last found something that is truly useful and beneficial. The Dharma heals. It is the best medicine, and the more we take that medicine, the more our trust in its wonderful properties will grow. With each passing day, our appreciation of the Buddhist teachings increases as our mind begins to change. That is what it's like to be directly introduced to the impermanent nature of all things. The realization hits us hard and brings us abruptly out of our sleep. The facts are painful at first, but sadness gives way to a dawning clarity.

Moved by deep joy, we think: *Finally, I have a sense of what it's all about. This change in me is enormous. Now I know how to eradicate confusion and suffering; I know how to be free. I feel so rich, and the road lies open before me. How wonderful!*

MATURING

When embarking on the path of Dharma, the mind shifts back and forth between joy and sadness. However, this process gradually matures the mind and makes us flexible, just like a child growing up. But if we really want to leave our spiritual childhood behind, the instructions have to hit home. It's only when they pierce our heart that things begin to happen.

UP AND DOWN

Usually it doesn't take much—in fact, it takes almost nothing—for us to lose our grip. If we become just a little bit well known, or if people begin to praise us, we are in heaven right away. When we have money, we feel so cool and unbeatable. When life is good, there's no end to how great we feel, but if suddenly things begin to hurt a bit, we feel as if our life is no longer worth living. When depressed, we feel like total failures, complete losers. Without social status, fame, and money, we just can't take it—until the tide changes and we once again feel on top of the world.

We could call this moodiness, but it's actually more like a bipolar disorder: one moment we are up in the clouds, and the next we are heading for the gloomy pits. When things go our way, we become manic. *Yes! Life is awesome; I am awesome!* But, really, what is so awesome? Everything and everyone might cease to be at any moment, but still, right now, we feel that it is all great and awesome. Then, when our mania fades, we despair and life just isn't worth living.

Until we reach awakening, we will keep shifting back and forth between mania and depression; there's no way around it. We know the characteristics of mania and depression, and we know their shortcomings. But when our emotions tighten their grip on us, it is almost impossible not to be carried away.

LOVE AND INSIGHT

Only love and insight will remedy this. Love and insight are characteristics of a mature mind, and we can grow up only by taking to heart the painful truth of impermanence. As long as we have not acknowledged the impermanent nature of things, we continue to be fickle and unreliable. The encounter with impermanence awakens us abruptly, but until that happens, we're like passed-out drunks. The awareness of impermanence gets us going and makes us progress. For a Dharma practitioner, there is no greater inspiration than impermanence.

TAME YOUR MIND

We have highlighted the importance of understanding that nothing lasts. The world we live in, our own body, and any amount of money, possessions, fame, and the like—everything will disappear. Everything changes from moment to moment. So, what do you do? Let go and set yourself free; become independent!

It's all a matter of training the mind, and the essence of this training is change—transformation. We need to train our minds and change ourselves on the mental, verbal, and physical levels. But in the end, everything stands and falls with the mind. Therefore, mental progress should be our top priority.

We may say: *I have recited millions of mantras! Look at my progress!* But can we really measure spiritual progress by counting? *I meditate five hours every day!* Sure, that's training all right. But does that necessarily mean that we have broken free and moved on? There's no guarantee. Genuine practice changes us from within, making our minds supple and flexible. Spending twenty years meditating in a mountain cave hardly qualifies as "progress" if our minds are still rigid and follow the same old rut. Perhaps it would have been better just to set aside a few hours a day for contemplating impermanence.

In the end, taming the mind is our own responsibility. Nobody can do it for us, not even the Buddha. That's why the Buddha said: "I show you the path to liberation, but whether you follow it is up to you."

Love

THE SEEMING AND THE REAL

The study of the Dharma is for the purpose of realizing reality, the true nature of all things. With that insight, all our negative emotions and obscurations disappear. But we also need to know what the world looks like from the perspective of others. In other words, we need to understand the world in all its endless complexity while at the same time never forgetting the reality that is its nature. That's the kind of insight we must aim for.

It's important that we understand both dimensions: reality as it appears to others and reality as it actually is. Knowing how others perceive the world is very valuable. We can't simply write off what others experience as "wrong" and leave it at that. Seen from the awakened perspective, the way ordinary beings perceive the world is indeed mistaken. But to us it's all very genuine.

No matter how confused and deluded we may be, we instinctively feel that our experience is real. That's why Buddhism talks about two aspects of reality: the seeming and the real. The seeming reality is certainly not irrelevant, because it's intuitively taken to be real.

THE BUDDHA'S PATH

On the other hand, if we take a closer look, we find that what otherwise seemed true and real is, in fact, neither. That discovery enables us to gain insight into the nature of things. We need to strike a delicate balance. We must acknowledge the way things appear but at the same time remain open and ready to recognize the way things actually are.

How do we make it work? First, we receive teachings and explanations, and we reflect deeply on what we hear. This way we arrive at a clear understanding of what the Dharma is actually about. The next step is to train in letting our newly acquired knowledge inform our lives. We need to apply our understanding in practical and concrete ways as we go through life. That is the only way to gain direct experience of the teachings. This is the Buddha's path to insight, openness, and realization.

SCRIPTURE AND REALIZATION

The type of instruction we receive and the kind of methods we employ will depend on who we are and how we work best. Dharma has two components: scripture, which refers to the teachings of the Buddha as they have been transmitted through the ages, and realization, which is the insight that unfolds through study and practice. First we listen, then we examine and reflect on what we heard, and finally we apply our understanding in practical contexts. For this process to succeed, we also need a foundation in ethics and a sense of discipline.

VOWS, ETHICS, AND DISCIPLINE

Ethical discipline entails a commitment to living life in the most constructive way possible. Buddhism provides different sets of vows that can assist us in this process. Buddhism's three major vehicles of teaching—the foundational vehicle, the great vehicle, and the vajra vehicle—each have their own specific vows, and there is a huge body of literature on the distinctions among these vehicles and the details of their vows.

Nevertheless, the three categories of vows can fortunately also be described in more general terms. If we can avoid causing other beings any kind of pain or distress, then we are keeping the vows of the foundational vehicle, which are focused on achieving freedom for ourselves. Next, if we not only avoid hurting others but also work for their benefit and happiness, then we are keeping the vows of the great vehicle, which is committed to bringing all beings to the awakened state. Finally, if we additionally acknowledge the fundamental purity of all things and if we are capable of living in accord with that realization, then we are keeping the vows of the vajra vehicle that bring complete awakening in this very life.

Whether we receive teachings, reflect on what we have heard, or apply our understanding in practical contexts, it is important that we do so while following those three aspects of ethical commitment.

MANY APPROACHES

The instructions and explanations we receive are always adjusted to suit our individual disposition and capacity for understanding. Each of us has our own individual perspective on the world, and all such individual perceptions and beliefs matter. Although mistaken with respect to the way things actually are, we still need to take our experience of the world into consideration. That's why there are many different

Buddhist philosophical traditions. They address people's distinct interests, beliefs, and abilities.

A COMMITMENT TO TRUTH

People often ask me if Buddhism is a religion or a philosophy. Buddhism may look like a religion or a philosophy, but in fact it is neither. Buddhism is a commitment to truth. The purpose of Buddhism is to understand and experience things as they really are. When we dedicate ourselves to this, we become Buddhists. Buddhism is not a religious or a philosophical project. Some people call Buddhism a religion because as Buddhists we seek refuge in the Three Jewels: the Buddha, the Dharma, and the Sangha. But in the end, the only reason we seek refuge is that we seek the realization of the way things actually are. That's why we rely on the Buddha, the source of wisdom; the Dharma, the teachings of awakening; and the Sangha, the community of people committed to the realization we are seeking.

STEP-BY-STEP

The Three Jewels—Buddha, Dharma, and Sangha—are actually our only real support. It doesn't matter how healthy, fit, successful, wealthy, intelligent, respected, or renowned we may be—one day it will all suddenly be gone, and everything will be different. We know this quite well already, but we prefer not to think about it. Still, what will we do when one day the rug is pulled from under our feet? Sure, we can pray to gods and guardian angels, but as the Buddha advises, we shouldn't have unrealistic expectations. There is a limit to the amount of help we can receive, even from an awakened buddha.

The Buddha promised to show us how we can free ourselves from our ignorance, delusion, destructive emotions, and suffering. His instructions are easy to understand and to apply, and the effects are concrete. But we also have to do our part of the job. The Buddha can show us how, but he can't do it all for us. The Buddha shows us the path, but we need to move forward, step-by-step. That's just the way it is.

RELIGION AND SCIENCE

These days, religion is a sensitive issue. In the past, religion used to play a significant role in people's daily lives, but nowadays the picture is more mixed. Some people think that religion is plain evil. Others think that it's a relic of the past, irrelevant in the contemporary world. There are also those who think that religion holds people in such a powerful grip that it's better just to play along and pretend to be a believer. Other people take their religion very, very seriously, thinking that their particular beliefs are the only true faith. Such people usually have little knowledge of other religions, yet they insist that everybody must believe what they themselves believe.

A central theme in many religions is the belief in an almighty and omniscient power that we cannot meet face-to-face, a sort of transcendent principle or being that sees everything we do, knows everything about us, and is capable of the most amazing feats. We, on the other hand, remain unable to hear or see this all-powerful entity. Through the ages, variations on this idea have become foundational in many religions, but the rise of science has increasingly challenged such convictions. It's not easy for a scientifically minded person to believe in an omnipresent god or divine power whose existence defies logic and cannot be verified through our senses.

Science has produced remarkable and life-changing discoveries and inventions that have made life easier and more comfortable. Even something like traveling from one place to another is altogether different and much less time-consuming than in the past. Science has no gods, yet it has granted us so many boons that it is hard for us not to place our trust in science. Even if we try to avoid trusting science, the marvelous effects of scientific thinking are still right in our face.

Of course, science is also responsible for many unfortunate things—just think about all the deadly weapons that were once inconceivable but are now part of our world. Still, many people believe more in science than religion. From a Buddhist perspective, that's actually OK—as Buddhists, aren't we always encouraged to investigate things carefully and objectively, just as scientists attempt to do?

BUDDHISM HAS NO DOGMA

We need to investigate things carefully and objectively—and that also goes for the Dharma. We shouldn't think that Buddhism is the absolute truth and that doubting it would be a sin. On the contrary, our task is to be critical. The Buddha said, "Monks, when you listen to my words, you must examine them carefully, like a skilled goldsmith who tests gold by heating, cutting, and rubbing. Do not accept my words merely out of respect."

The Buddha tells us that we shouldn't accept his words just because they are his. This sets Buddhism apart from many other religions. Some religions consider it a sin to question anything at all that is taught in their holy scriptures. Other religions may encourage their followers to investigate things a bit more closely, but only up to a point. And if we happen to cross the line, we'll soon find out. . . .

However, in Buddhism there is no limit to what we may question. There are no dogmas that must remain unchallenged. This is a special feature of the Buddhist teaching and the Buddhist path. Practicing the Dharma is a hands-on, concrete activity that begins by observing the world and ourselves.

IMPERMANENCE

For example, we will notice that no matter what we may build, it's just a matter of time before it falls apart. We all know the urge to create something, and we may work really hard to make our wishes come true. Yet no matter how skilled or hardworking we are, whatever we may succeed in building or assembling will sooner or later disappear. That's just the way it is, and there's nothing we can do about it. When we meet, it's just a matter of time before we will part ways again. No two people can stay together forever. Our money in the bank will also be gone one day. This is the nature of conditioned existence.

CRADLE TO GRAVE

Deep down we know it very well: birth ends in death, and that goes for every one of us. Whoever enters this world is doomed to leave it again. We're all in different phases of our lives. Some of us are young, some are middle-aged, and some are old. Some are in what could poetically be called life's sunset. Yet none of us knows how many years we have left. Death can come to anyone at any time—that is certain—but we have absolutely no idea when it will come. The only thing we know for a fact is that at some point we will die.

ACTION

Many of the things we keep in mind as Buddhists are actually quite banal. But they are nevertheless very helpful because they give us the sense that we'd better make something of our lives while we still have the chance. Otherwise, while we wait, time quietly runs out. Life is over before we know it. But the thought of impermanence urges us to seize the moment and discover what's going on and what Buddhism is really about. Not just as dry, intellectual knowledge, but also in a way that really makes a difference in our lives. We need an insight that causes us to break free from all the misguided thoughts and ideas that otherwise distort our perception of things. We need a breakthrough that allows us to let go of all the emotions that keep pushing us from one miserable situation to another.

FREEDOM

A breakthough is exactly what the Buddha's teachings are here to deliver. The Buddha demonstrated true freedom and the way to experience it. Genuine freedom is absolute freedom—a freedom from emotions, a freedom that doesn't belong to anyone, a freedom that we can share with all beings. The Buddha showed us a path that ultimately transforms an ordinary person into an awakened buddha—someone who has conquered all there is to conquer, has accomplished all there is to accomplish, and is capable of communicating this wisdom to others.

CHANGE, PAIN, AND PROGRESS

Everything we experience is in a process of change. Each and every thing we see, hear, smell, taste, or touch is changing from one moment to the next. That also goes for all that we have achieved in this life—wealth, enjoyments, status. They may be ours for a while, but then they evaporate. There's nothing in this world that we can actually rely on. And deep down we know that perfectly well.

We do know that conditioned things are impermanent—everything that exists due to causes is bound to disappear—but it's scary to think about it. All that we love and cherish will be gone—what a painful, sad recognition. Yet it's a necessary one. Not because we want to sit with melancholic tears in our eyes, but because this acknowledgment calls us to action. It inspires us toward awakening.

THE REMEDY

Whether we like it or not, all things that exist because of other things are impermanent. We need to take that into account, because that's how it is. As Dharma practitioners, we have a remedy: we can break the mind's conditioning that otherwise holds us to a perception of things that is neither constructive nor enjoyable for anyone. We can do away with the ignorance that produces the experience of a painful world—it's a real option. As practitioners, we acknowledge the facts and act upon them. That's what an ordinary person fails to do.

SPIRITUAL TRAINING

Sooner or later, we all have to face change and impermanence. There will come a day when the world reveals its impermanent nature, and then we encounter the painful, sad facts first-hand. That type of experience hits ordinary people very hard. It's also hard for practitioners, but there is a big difference. Practitioners know what to do in the situation; they aren't left with only a painful recognition. They have a remedy, and the remedy is spiritual training.

HAVING A CHOICE

There are many ways to train. For example, we can just work on developing an attitude toward our surroundings that is less rigid and more open and accommodating. That's one simple, effective remedy. It's important to understand that the basic facts remain the same, whether or not we are practitioners. But Dharma practitioners have a choice: they don't have to merely register the painful facts; they can actually do something about them.

HEART OF STONE

How do you feel when you realize that everything around you will disappear, that nothing lasts? Doesn't it make you sad? If you think: *Oh well, what to do, that's the way the world is,* then you haven't really thought through what this truly means. If you think deeply about impermanence, it is impossible not to be struck by a deep sorrow. If things were different, if things actually lasted, then it would be ridiculous to sit around and think that everything is going to disappear. But we just need to open our eyes and look around to see that is not the case. We won't be in doubt.

Everything we see, hear, and experience changes character from moment to moment. So-and-so is now ill; so-and-so has now died. Such-and-such is withering; such-and-such is fading; such-and-such is no more. It hurts to notice all this, no matter who we are. If we allow ourselves to reflect on the impermanence of everyone and everything, a profound sense of sorrow sets in; it would take a heart of stone to remain unaffected.

DEPRESSION

News comes to us about people falling ill and dying. We learn that suddenly people can't seem to get along. We find that things have been destroyed, broken, and torn apart. In such cases, the underlying reason is always impermanence. And impermanence hurts. But we need to recognize life for what it is. That's the only way we can develop an approach to life that is realistic as well as constructive. In fact, if all the pain and sorrow seem paralyzing, we haven't quite gotten it yet. Getting stuck is getting it wrong. Getting stuck means getting depressed, and becoming depressed just makes a tough situation worse. So, we need an approach that recognizes the fact of impermanence but uses it as an opportunity to develop the qualities of love and insight.

COURAGE

For that to happen, we first need courage to face pain and sorrow openly and honestly. Everything changes, including ourselves, those around us, and all that we own. The people we have known, loved, and lived with will not remain with us. The things we value and consider ours, even our standing and status in society—none of it will remain. Things change, but nobody can say exactly when or how. Those are basic facts of life.

Change just comes to us, and there's nothing we can do to halt it. Therefore, we need to see the world as it is, and we must know how to relate constructively to pain and impermanence.

SUFFERING

In Buddhism we hear a lot about suffering, but people often misunderstand what that really means. Suffering isn't just about sickness, starvation, and poverty. Of course, those are aspects of suffering, but suffering in the Buddhist sense goes much deeper. In the Buddhist understanding, we're always confronted with suffering, no matter how much or little we own or how sick or healthy we are. Suffering means to be controlled by hope and fear, over and over, again and again. *That* is suffering! In a moment of clarity, we realize that we have no clue what might happen just five minutes from now. Everything is uncertain and doubtful. We have no idea what life may have in store for us.

ALL FOR NOTHING

There is only one cure for suffering, and that is practice. Wealth and fame won't solve this problem. Intelligence, power, and influence can't help us either. Human history abounds with kings and emperors, and presidents and heads of state who ruled over vast realms yet were ultimately forced to surrender to impermanence. Take a moment to think how they must have felt. Some even took their own lives. They conquered, ruled, and decreed, but in the end what did they get out of it? They couldn't keep anything at all. We are powerless against impermanence. Family, friends, merit, and intelligence—nothing can protect us. Whether we are doctors, scientists, politicians, or business people, all of us must capitulate when facing impermanence. The only real source of help is our attitude, which can be developed through meditation practice.

PANIC

As soon as we begin thinking about impermanence, panic creeps in and we think: *One day I will be separated from all my loved ones! No matter what I build or gather, I can't keep any of it! Nothing lasts. I can't trust anything!*

It really is terribly sad, and thinking about it hurts. We'd rather not consider or talk about impermanence. We'd prefer to forget all about it as soon as possible. We certainly don't want to look at death, deal with death, or talk about death! When something is unpleasant and painful, we want it to disappear instantly. Nobody wants to hold on to a source of pain. On the other hand, whenever we find something that is enjoyable and gives us pleasure, we want to keep it as long as possible, preferably forever. We pick flowers and arrange them in a vase, but when they are no longer fresh and beautiful, we throw them away because their ugliness turns us off. We wish only to enjoy their beauty and lovely scent. But ugliness doesn't suddenly descend onto the flowers. Ugliness, decay, and the smell of rot are just as intrinsic to the flowers as their beauty. All are equally the results of impermanence.

SADNESS, OUR FRIEND

If we don't practice meditation, impermanence will be our worst enemy. But if we do, that same impermanence becomes our best friend. As we develop our understanding of impermanence, we discover calm. With balance and calm, there naturally comes a greater capacity for love and care. We can afford to be caring, and as we become increasingly kindhearted and responsive to others, our minds brighten. Insight into the way things really are grows from loving care. Love nurtures wisdom.

Understanding impermanence is the basis for all that is good, wholesome, joyful, and great. In that way, impermanence is our greatest teacher and our foremost source of inspiration. Coming to terms with impermanence involves sorrow and pain, but if that sadness becomes deeply integrated in our lives, we will definitely become exemplary practitioners. That's guaranteed. On the other hand, if the sadness is with us only sometimes, and to a limited extent, then we are only halfhearted practitioners. Moreover, if this feeling is weak and rarely present in our minds, then we resemble practitioners only occasionally, but most of the time not at all.

If we ignore the impermanence of things, it's easy to lose all connection with the Dharma. It becomes simply uninteresting. In fact, ignoring impermanence is a characteristic of people who do not practice. Dharma practitioners, on the other hand, continuously remind themselves about the impermanence of all things, and appreciate it, because they know how important that awareness is. Please don't underestimate the significance of understanding impermanence. It's a crucial subject.

PERSEVERANCE

To practitioners, impermanence is a kind friend, but to ordinary people it's their archenemy, someone who keeps hurting them. That's why it is so important to be aware of impermanence—to bring it to mind and take it to heart. We need to consider impermanence as our guru, our teacher. As soon as we forget about impermanence, we lose our focus and become distracted by a lot of things that make us lose sight of what is truly important. Our practice becomes halfhearted and we put it off.

When I was a young student, my teachers would often speak to us about impermanence. It made me feel uneasy and sad, and I found the topic both boring and irritating. Often I just didn't want to hear about it at all. Today, I realize how those teachings have helped me.

FAITH

Faith is quite a sensitive issue. Most people find the idea of compassion compelling, but *faith*? Why would we want faith? But as Buddhists we tell each other to have faith in the Three Jewels. Faith begins with trust, because there's something we have become clear about. In Buddhism, we need to become clear about dependent origination. That clarity automatically leads to faith. Once we have really understood dependent origination, we cannot help feeling faith. It wells up inside us, whether we like it or not. Dependent origination is a crucial issue.

People who are not religious often regard religious beliefs and convictions as mere superstitions, and they feel a kind of pity for those who subscribe to them. Meanwhile, religious people pity nonbelievers, thinking of them as lost souls. So, everybody pities each other, back and forth.

Faith in a Buddhist context lies between these two positions. Buddhist faith arises through understanding, and what we need to understand is dependent origination and impermanence. It can be very simply put: Buddhist faith arises as one becomes clear about the links that constitute these processes.

FROM IMPERMANENCE TO COMPASSIONATE WISDOM

We have talked about impermanence and how painful it is to acknowledge that everything, including ourselves and all that we love, is going to perish. But the recognition of impermanence is also the threshold to something more, something greater. The reason we take impermanence to heart is that we need that understanding to inspire and guide us. Impermanence closes the gap between others and ourselves. When we recognize that everyone is subject to the same merciless conditions, we cannot but respond with affection. With the recognition of the impermanent world comes great compassion, genuine care. This pivotal discovery provides the circumstance for a complete opening of our minds. As compassion gains force, it enables our minds to recognize the profound nature of emptiness—the true nature of things that lies beyond all concepts. Sorrow and pain become catalysts for deep-felt loving care, and the power of universal compassion delivers the realization of the true view. That's when we have truly become students of the Dharma.

LOVE AND COMPASSION FOR ALL

Understanding impermanence makes it possible for us to regard all beings with love and compassion. Genuine love and compassion are not intended only for certain individuals, groups, or categories of beings. Genuine love and compassion embrace everyone. True love and compassion are all-encompassing, unconditional, and sincere. The more love and compassion we have within us, the more natural it will be to realize the true nature of things. The liberating insight into the way things really are begins to unfold from within. When the realization of impermanence has set us free so that there is a welling up inside us of love and compassion for all beings, true insight will expand and grow by itself.

NATURAL PRESENCE

What is true insight? What is the view that recognizes reality, the true nature of all things? And what is our own true nature? Actually, we all possess the awakened state within us, as a natural endowment. So, when we refer to the Buddha as the "awakened one," we are actually talking about something that we ourselves have always possessed. The awakened qualities and wisdom are naturally and spontaneously present within us—and that presence can be recognized through the right view. The very essence of awakening is not something extrinsic to us. We possess it already and can never lose it, even if we wanted to. The awakened state is present in all beings, whether they appreciate it or not.

That is the right view, true insight. But if we want genuine insight to unfold, we will need universal love and compassion. These two qualities arise naturally and spontaneously when we take impermanence to heart. When in that way we arrive at the genuine view, we become capable of communicating this liberating realization to others, skillfully and compassionately. At that point, we finally become a loving servant, savior, and friend to all beings. All that is required for this to happen is that we set the process in motion.

HOW DO WE HELP OTHERS?

When we talk about love and compassion, it's important that we understand what's behind the words. In Buddhism, the objects of our love and compassion are all beings. And "all" really means *all*. But how do we help all beings? We must begin by examining what we can actually do for others. Let's ask ourselves what we can do to remove their pain, be it physical or mental, and how we can give them joy and well-being, both in the present and also from a long-term perspective. If we want to practice love and compassion toward all beings, we need to understand that the best way to help is through developing wisdom.

THE MIND OF AWAKENING

One way we can be of help to others is actually just a matter of thinking like this: *I want to help all beings. I want to liberate them from all types of suffering and give them all that is good and meaningful.*

This intention, called *the mind of awakening*, known in Sanskrit as *bodhicitta*, possesses tremendous power. When we begin to think in this way—when we sincerely wish to help and protect all beings—then all our negative thoughts and emotions automatically disappear. They simply cannot coexist with the mind of awakening.

With the mind of awakening, it becomes impossible to be selfish. We cannot be envious, and there is no way that we would want to deceive or compete with anyone. The basis for malice and resentment is gone. This change is natural and undeniable. Once our coarse, negative thoughts and emotions disappear, we will automatically be of use and benefit to others.

TWO THOUGHTS

There is infinitely much that we might possibly think and feel. Myriads of different thoughts and ideas run through our minds. But among all the thoughts that we might possibly have, there are two that stand out as truly special. The first is the thought of impermanence. Thinking about impermanence clears the mind of its clutter. It enables us to think of and perceive the world in a way that is radically different and genuinely constructive. The second is love and compassion. Love and compassion hold inconceivable power. Love and compassion never lead us astray. Love and compassion strip the mind of negative emotions and unwholesome thoughts. Dharma practice is about recognizing impermanence so that love and compassion become all-encompassing and universal.

THE DIRECT PATH

All-encompassing love and compassion are incredibly powerful. The goodness they bring is tremendous—simply unimaginable. That's why the mind of awakening, the sincere wish to help others, is considered such an important factor for the path—it heals and restores. When we are loving and compassionate, none of our selfish tendencies or negative emotions can find any bearing. Our consciousness is purified and we can begin to think constructively. The mind of awakening allows us to care for others, giving them genuine joy and happiness, as well as true protection from suffering.

But let's remember that all these wonderful qualities emerge only if we devote our love and compassion to *all* beings. Our love and compassion cannot be limited to our friends, family, and the people we already care about. We must extend our love and compassion to everyone, including strangers and even those who seek to harm us. If we can do that, there is no better way to go through life. The mind of awakening has infinite wonderful qualities, and it leads us directly to freedom and true awakening.

INTELLIGENT LOVE AND COMPASSION

Love and compassion must be paired with insight. Without intelligence, it's hard to be of real benefit to others. Obviously, we can help others in a limited manner, but we cannot accomplish anything that has truly far-reaching positive consequences. That's possible only when loving-kindness and insight combine and mutually enrich each other. Love and compassion should arise and unfold based on insight and understanding, just as wisdom should be nourished and fueled by loving care. When that happens, our practice really takes off.

BOUNDLESS LOVE AND COMPASSION

Boundless love and compassion are unlimited and all-embracing. They extend to all beings. How are we to understand "all"? Again, "all" really means *all*. Could there be a love and compassion more true and real than that—a loving compassion that embraces *every single being*? That's the kind of love and compassion we must cultivate. When we feel equal love and compassion for everyone, near or far, whoever they are, then our practice is authentic. But that doesn't happen by itself. As beginners, we need to cultivate such a frame of mind, and we must stay alert to make sure it doesn't disappear.

HEALTHY MINDS

The more trained we become, the less effort we need. As long as we actively cultivate love and compassion, as long as it's a conscious, deliberate activity, for that long our practice will require a certain measure of effort. Nonetheless, even as we train in that way, we remain in a state that is thoroughly good and wholesome. When our love and compassion are warm and strong no matter whom we encounter, the very basis for harming others disappears. Any inclination to hurt others is gone.

Then everything we do springs from a wish to help and support others; our only wish is to make them happy, now and forever. There is no evil, no negativity. Here we can really talk about a healthy mind, a consciousness that abounds with positive qualities and lets insight unfold naturally.

SPONTANEOUS LOVE AND COMPASSION

When there is no negativity, animosity, or selfishness in our minds, realization unfolds by itself. We reach a point where insight into the true nature of things occurs naturally, without any effort on our part. Then, once we see things as they really are and become aware of their actual nature, we begin to experience love and compassion at a level that is absolutely unparalleled. All-embracing love and compassion arise freely and without effort. That's what the teachings describe so beautifully, but at this point it's actually happening, all by itself. We don't need to do anything; universal love and compassion just well up in us. When Buddhism talks about "great love and compassion," that's what is meant. This is what we are training to achieve.

THAT ONE THING

Generally, we're not intimidated by hard work, whether it's physical or mental. That's because we want so much to be happy. This is true of all beings. No matter who we are or how we live our lives, everyone wants to improve on their current situation. Obviously, this is particularly true for people who don't know about Dharma, but let's be honest: we're all that way, aren't we? As soon as we get the sense that something can make us happy, we begin to work toward it with discipline and perseverance. The road may be long and full of trials, but we just toughen up and soldier on. We insist on finding happiness, no matter the cost.

Some people have a clear idea about what it takes for them to be happy. It may be a certain job or title, or it might be fame, recognition, or simply to be known by a lot of people. For others it might be privilege and luxury. Whatever it is we wish for ourselves, we get the feeling that only that, and nothing else, is what will satisfy us.

SAD IRONY

The irony is rather tragic because our quest for happiness rarely brings us anything but suffering and negativity. As we strive to reach our goals, other people are reduced to extras on our stage, if not outright obstacles to be eliminated. We do things that we didn't think we would ever consider. The end justifies the means, as they say.

That's how the world operates, and sometimes, much to our delight, we do succeed in getting our hands on the things we wanted. The problem, however, is that the happiness we feel then tends to be very short-lived. We have sweated and toiled, yet somehow, we have a sneaking feeling that now the real work is only beginning, just when we thought it was time to lean back and enjoy the fruits of our labor. That is because nothing can be trusted. Impermanence is tough; maintaining something requires at least as much effort as acquiring it in the first place. This is not merely unsatisfying—it's actually tragic. Obtaining something we have striven for is painfully meaningless unless we are able to enjoy it once we finally have it. Instead, we feel we have to be on guard all the time, just to prevent it from disappearing.

Another thing that makes life miserable is our instinctive tendency to conjure up new wishes and needs. As soon as we have achieved one thing, we immediately start thinking about something else that we can't live without. That way, we never manage to appreciate and enjoy what is here right now. That's how life is—at least for people who have no clue about Dharma practice.

A DIFFERENT PATH

Dharma practitioners also look for happiness, but at the same time they remain disciplined and determined. Their search for happiness is therefore different. Dharma practitioners look for the very *source* of joy and happiness, and that source is found within us. Joy and happiness depend on three inner qualities—the wish to be free, loving-kindness, and insight. When these three factors are present in our minds, joy and happiness will always naturally follow. When the wish to be free, loving-kindness, and insight become our inner compass, our journey will surely be a happy one.

Since Dharma practitioners search for a different kind of happiness, they also follow a different path. The Dharma doesn't lead us from one miserable situation to the next. The path of Dharma goes from joy to happiness, and not just personal, private happiness. The joy that is inspired by the Dharma is for the good of all beings. When we rely on love and insight, we ensure that our presence in this world benefits others. A warm and benevolent heart motivates all that we do. We wish that everyone may recognize and experience the qualities that are the source of true happiness and freedom from suffering, now and forever.

When love and compassion become genuinely universal, they prevent us from acting in ways that harm anyone, including ourselves. Anger, selfishness, pride, and envy vanish like dewdrops in the morning sun. Genuine loving care benefits everyone. When loving-kindness resides in our hearts, we will always make the right choices and move in the right direction, no matter what is our situation. Loving care for everyone is the source of happiness, now and in the future.

THE QUALITIES OF COMPASSION

Great compassion speaks the truth and is never hypocritical. Great compassion does not hurt or deceive. Great compassion cares lovingly for others without any negative emotions or hidden agendas. Great compassion never leads us astray. When it wells up in us, we simply lose the capacity for malice, and everything we do is aimed at helping, healing, and comforting.

Love and compassion are the source of true awakening. Genuine love and care for others are the qualities that purify all obscurations, dispel all obstacles, and dissolve all negative emotions. Love and compassion solve all problems and unlock all difficult situations. In short, love and compassion are the source of all that is good.

PREREQUISITES

For our training to become genuine and effective, we need the wish for liberation. This enables us to break free from the cycle of life and death, and it builds a foundation for developing true love. As our love and compassion become constant, genuine, and pure, the awakened state will dawn like the rising sun. Without love and compassion, all our efforts would ultimately be in vain.

STAINS ON THE MIRROR

Without love and compassion, the mind is impure. Right now, our minds are like a mirror covered with smudges and streaks. When we look into the mirror, the image is blurred. But if we clean the mirror, it's easy to see that the mirror itself was never unclean. The same is true of our minds. The actual nature of the mind is pure and clear. That goes for everyone, from the tiniest insect to an awakened buddha. The true nature of the mind is pure and clear, but unlike the mind of an

awakened buddha, our pure and clean minds are continuously stained by negative emotions. To remove those stains,
we need love and compassion.

LIVING PRACTICE

Earlier, I mentioned how sorrow and weariness can help us
to let go and break free from the cycle of life and death. That
type of sadness is necessary, as it enriches us and widens our
outlook. Such healthy sadness grows from contemplating
the impermanent nature of everything around us. I have also
mentioned the importance of giving rise to love and compassion. Reflecting on love and compassion is worthwhile because they should be our basic motivation in all that we do. It's
not just when we sit on our meditation cushion that we need
love and compassion. We need to be loving and compassionate when we are eating our meals, sitting on the toilet, having
a good time, working, talking on the phone, and relaxing. In
short, we need to remember our practice always, no matter
where we are!

Remember your practice at all times, from when you
wake up until you go to bed—in fact, even while you sleep.
That way, your body will become the retreat cabin in which
your mind can practice. For that to happen, we need to watch
the mind because it is always up to new tricks. We constantly
get distracted by work, entertainment, computers, and mes-
sages. Then we develop stress and attend seminars on "mindfulness"—but what does it really mean to be mindful? To be
mindful is to remind oneself. And what did the Buddha ask us
to remember? Love and insight.

MINDFULNESS, ALERTNESS, AND CAREFULNESS

To remember love and insight, we need three tools: mindfulness, alertness, and carefulness. In Buddhism we make use of these three methods, but it's important to remember that they aren't ends in themselves. They are just tools. Mindfulness means keeping in mind how to practice. Alertness means being aware of everything that goes on around us. Carefulness is being judicious about all that we do physically, verbally, and mentally.

We depend on mindfulness, alertness, and carefulness to become clear about impermanence, to let our love and compassion grow, and to make our insight authentic. The wish to be free, loving-kindness, and insight—that's what it's all about. These are the very essence of the Buddha's teachings. Mindfulness, alertness, and carefulness are the means whereby we awaken and strengthen those vital qualities.

What happens when we make use of mindfulness, alertness, and carefulness? We become less confused, more relaxed, and more grounded. Our negative emotions arise less frequently, and we become more loving, compassionate, and bright.

BUDDHIST "THERAPY"?

Buddhist practice works incredibly well. The Dharma has tremendous power, as long as we get off on the right foot and follow through. So, it's not that helpful to single out any one technique, remove it from its traditional context, and then make a big deal about it. If we do that, it's very easy to miss the actual point.

Unfortunately, this happens quite a lot these days. People stumble upon a Buddhist technique and advertise it as some particular "therapy." The real significance and context of the practice is deliberately toned down, and instead it is presented as a groundbreaking "scientific" discovery. People love that kind of thing, and with a bit of luck it's also possible to get rich and famous that way. But the fact is that the unique methods of Buddhism are presented to the general public out of context and without proper training. That's not a service to anyone.

THE DARK AGE

The Buddha spoke of a future "dark" age when the elements of nature become imbalanced and cause great harm. New diseases will appear, new types of weapons will be invented, and so on. The Buddha also described the dark age as a time when all that is natural and authentic loses importance and instead people worship what is artificial and false. This applies to people as well as to things.

We now live in a time when people with good and healthy qualities, who have meaningful things to say, rarely get much attention. At the same time, people who have nothing much to offer speak to sold-out crowds. People aren't interested in the real thing, but if we can come up with something that *seems* like the real deal, then it becomes popular right away. The same goes for the food we eat. People rarely appreciate genuine, natural ingredients. We prefer products that are processed, artificial, and, most important, cheap. Everywhere we are surrounded by products that are artificial and cheap, while the genuine, uncontaminated, and authentic is becoming rare. We live in the twenty-first century, and we like to think of ourselves as modern, sophisticated, and civilized. But honestly, what kind of civilization pays tribute to things that are fake, cheap, and contaminated?

A CIVILIZED WORLD?

We live in a time when technology increasingly controls our lives. We have invested technology with so much power that we can no longer survive without all its comforts. We started this process ourselves, and now we struggle to keep up. Day by day, we become increasingly insignificant. Compared with the force of the all-powerful weapons that exist today, we are nothing, even less than ants. And yet those weapons were not made by demons or aliens from another planet. They were made by humans just like me and you.

The weapons are here to protect us, we might say, but that's a false confidence. If we ever press the red button, others will do the same. If we bomb them, bombs will rain on us. That's cause and effect, and it will just go on and on. So what can we do? Only one thing can help us: loving-kindness. Loving-kindness is the very foundation of a civilized world.

Openness

SELFLESSNESS

I would like to stress once again how crucial it is to have the right motivation in the context of Dharma practice. Whether we are listening, reading, practicing, translating, or simply helping out, whatever we do in relation to the Dharma should always be done with the sincere wish to help and protect others. Don't hope for respect and admiration. Don't think of accumulating merit. In short, don't expect a reward. It might sound strange, but the less we care about recognition from others, the more recognized we will be, and our rewards will be that much greater.

THE NATURE OF MIND

Among people interested in Buddhism these days, there is an increasing desire to receive instructions that point out the nature of the mind. People may have read about such an introduction in books or on the internet. In any case, there's a lot of talk about "pointing out" or "introduction," but often people don't really know what that means. When people visit me in my monastery in Nepal, they sometimes ask, "Please introduce me to the nature of my mind! My plane leaves tomorrow morning, so I'm in a bit of a hurry!" It almost sounds as if they think the nature of mind is a special thing, a bit like a tourist attraction, which they have to see before they're off to the airport. On other occasions, people talk to me as if I were a gardener and the nature of mind were a rare flower that they want to see and smell.

The Buddha's teachings are one continuous introduction to the way things really are. So far, we have been introduced to impermanence and suffering: Nothing is reliable. Nothing lasts. Everything is fragile. Everything changes. The reason we spend so much time talking about impermanence and suffering is that our approach to life needs to change. This change happens naturally when we feel that we have encountered the truth. And it is true that there is nothing to rely on. The truth is that everything changes from moment to moment—fame, wealth, power, and privilege, as well as our health and friendships. The tides turn. The winds of fortune shift. Everything changes, always. Whenever we take a moment to pause, we realize that we already know this fact of life. That's a sign that the introduction to impermanence has hit home. Now we know. That is a powerful and crucial recognition.

So, let's not spend our lives fantasizing about a magic moment when our teacher introduces us to the nature of mind and we live happily ever after. Don't get me wrong—I'm not saying that the introduction to the nature of mind isn't important. It most certainly is important. In fact, it's crucial! But because it's so important, we should ask ourselves if we have truly understood the significance of impermanence and suffering. Do we actually get this profound message, and do we take its implications to heart? If not, then we're not going to benefit from teachings on the nature of mind, because we're simply not ready.

HUMILITY

Now that we have received the introduction to impermanence, we need to practice accordingly. So how do we incorporate impermanence in our practice? We keep in mind that there's nothing for us to rely on—this humbles us and grounds us. I know this from personal experience.

When I was a young child living in Tibet with my family, the monks at my monastery treated me as if I were a buddha. My mother used to warn me: "Be careful—you have not yet fully awakened. Unless you practice, you could end up in trouble!" Of course I respected my mother's advice, but it was only when I was forced to flee from violence and invasion that I became truly grounded. Overnight, my family lost everything and became beggars. We had no passports and nowhere to go. That experience really grounded me. It made me a better practitioner, and today I'm very grateful to the communists for introducing me to impermanence.

In other words, please don't think that your current circumstances won't ever change, because they will. Wealth dries up. We may be young and healthy, but sooner or later a serious disease will strike us—that is, if we are lucky enough even to live that long. Death can come at any time. Nothing is certain. Everything changes all the time. Of course, impermanence also sometimes means change is for the better—poverty can change to affluence, and diseases may be cured—but only for a while, because everything is temporary and nothing lasts. Right now we have a unique opportunity to let ourselves become intimately familiar with impermanence, because *now we know.*

TRIVIALITIES

We like to think that our existence somehow has a very profound purpose, but actually it's quite trivial. We are born, grow up, go to school, graduate, get a job, and make money. Maybe we marry, maybe we don't. Maybe we have kids, maybe we don't. But the basic routine is the same for all of us. We talk about the weather and attend important meetings. We make plans for the future and purchase the things we want. And so life passes. But if we suffuse our life with a spiritual outlook, we can go beyond its trivialities and give it a deeper meaning.

DISTRACTIONS

The more sophisticated we become, the less time we seem to have. Progress rarely allows us to relax. The more developed and civilized we are, the harder it is for us to live in a natural way. We become blind to the world around us. Trees, leaves, birds, and flowers—we hardly notice them. We rush around and rarely are truly present, even in the company of our friends and family. We're always occupied by something. And in those rare moments when we are able to slow down, the small portable gadgets we have invented make sure we stay busy and never notice what is right in front of us. That's life in the twenty-first century—wouldn't it be better to take back the reins from the many distractions we have created?

FROM GODS TO THINGS

In the past, people lived in a world inhabited by invisible beings and gods. These days, we have replaced them with things that can be measured, weighed, and counted. We want to create things, and we want to own, build, and invest. Yet our hopes and fears haven't diminished. In fact, they are stronger than ever. We worry more, and worries are suffering. Among all the different types of suffering, the worst is the pain we feel in our minds.

If we're not careful and we don't begin to see things for what they are, we risk becoming less caring, loving, and trusting. The more importance we place on our possessions, the more our relationships with others will suffer. We trust technology and money more than we trust those around us. We obsess about our career and forget our family.

ENEMY OF HAPPINESS

All our troubles come from the urge to take possession of things. That urge is the archenemy of happiness, an unwholesome impulse that causes conflict and disharmony. Desire and selfishness are mental weapons of mass destruction, and they are tearing our world apart, literally and figuratively. The Buddha warned us against them, but he also explained the origins of desire and selfishness and showed us how to break free of their grip. Now it's up to us to learn about the tools that are at our disposal.

SELF-DECEPTION

Often, when I hear people talking about receiving the introduction to the nature of mind, they make it sound like something unbelievably amazing, something magical. There is a tendency to believe that if only we can be introduced to the nature of mind, then we won't need anything else at all. And in a way, of course, it's true. When an authentic master introduces a qualified student to the nature of mind, nothing else is needed. Sometimes the mere meeting of master and disciple is enough for the student not only to recognize the nature of mind but also to gain stability in that recognition—even if the student has no prior knowledge of the Dharma. But such cases are more rare than stars in the midday sky.

That doesn't mean that it's impossible for people like us to recognize the nature of mind, because that's definitely possible. But a bit of honest self-appraisal would serve us well. We may seek out one master after another so that we can listen to some poetic, well-chosen words about the nature of mind, and it may also be that those words somehow strike a chord in us. But does that mean that we have actually experienced and recognized the nature of mind? Or was it simply an idea, a thought, or a mood that came over us? Things must be absolutely clear to both the master and student. Otherwise we're just fooling ourselves, and that won't get us anywhere.

LET GO

The introduction to impermanence is important. But it's just as important that we learn how to handle that knowledge, because there is hardly a more painful recognition. So now it's time for the next instruction. What do we do once we have recognized that nothing lasts? Here is a simple and effective technique: *Let go. Don't hold on so tightly. The more you let go, the less it hurts. Let go entirely and the pain is gone. On the other hand, the more we grasp, the more painful it is.*

That's a very clear, simple, and effective instruction. It's easy to understand, and we get the point. So now that we have gained that realization, it is up to us to make use of that insight. In any case, from this day on, we no longer need to wonder how to handle the pain when something ends, changes, ages, or disappears. Letting go is immediately applicable and more precious than gold. That is the first step.

A GOOD HEART

Next comes the introduction to love and compassion. We all need love and compassion. Without these two, we cannot even take care of ourselves. And if we are unable to take care of ourselves, then how could we ever manage to look after others? Love and compassion aren't just religious virtues. Everyone agrees that having a good heart is important, so having that view does not require believing in the Buddha, Dharma, and Sangha, nor is it necessary to believe in cause and effect, or in reincarnation, for that matter. It's a natural belief that we all share.

TWO KINDS OF LOVE

What makes a heart "good"? We like to talk about love, but often such talk is just fancy words. Behind the facade, our love mostly is anything but unconditional. Ordinary, romantic love is actually quite egoistic: *I love you, because you love me.*

The Buddha talked about *great* love and compassion. What is meant by "great"? At night, when everything is dark, even a tiny light shines brightly. Ordinary love is like a tiny light in the dark of night. But when the sun rises at dawn, it shines its light on every one of us. Great love is like the brilliant sun. No light shines brighter than that. Even if we lit every candle and turned on every electric light in this world, it would all pale in comparison to the brilliant light of the sun.

Great love burns with an incredible strength and intensity. It heals and purifies. All obscurations and destructive emotions disappear. Self-importance, greed, pride, doubt, and envy vanish, and all that is good appears. What is meant by "all that is good"? Goodness is honesty. Goodness is warmth and care. Goodness is insight and wisdom. When the mind is filled with love—true, unconditional love—it is naturally honest and pure. It happens automatically, no matter who we are or what we believe in.

WHO'S ON THE RIGHT PATH?

Having a pure, loving mind doesn't require being a religious person. I have met people who don't believe in any religion, who don't follow any religious practice, and yet they are one hundred percent honest and genuine. Such people are definitely on the right path. Their journey is pure and good. We might ask ourselves why they are so honest and sincere, and the answer is that their minds are pure. Their minds are pure because they are caring and loving. They do not want to hurt, harm, or cheat anyone. So their journey is good. They are on the right path. This is simple cause and effect.

On the other hand, it's also possible to be very religious, pious, and self-sacrificing but at the same time suffer from intense pride. When we suffer from pride, we feel that we are better and more worthy than others. When others succeed, we feel annoyed and envious. When we are not applauded and praised, we feel offended. We feel that if others don't recognize us and thank us for what we have done, then why should we even bother? Despite our piety and good deeds, we might remain very ordinary on the inside. That is why it is important to know what it really means to be on the right path.

ONE PATH

We need to maintain our practice at every moment, regardless of the circumstances. Our inspiration is impermanence and our means are love and compassion. Only through loving-kindness and insight into reality will we ever find true and lasting joy and the capacity to benefit both others and ourselves. Happiness and the cause of happiness can arise only through loving-kindness and insight into the nature of things. There is no other way.

Unless we understand this crucial point, there will be no end to our suffering. It doesn't matter how much we own or whether others respect us. It doesn't matter how influential we are or how lavishly we live. Life is always characterized by suffering. That's an innate flaw. We are unable to relax in the present moment, and we cannot appreciate things the way they are. Our anger, desire, and confusion stand between us and happiness.

TWO KINDS OF HAPPINESS

We all want happiness. Of course, people have their own particular ideas about what it means to be happy, but we all share the same basic wish to be happy. Now, roughly speaking, there are two types of happiness: conditioned and unconditioned. Unconditioned happiness refers to loving-kindness and insight. It is a state of spontaneous love and wisdom that realizes the great emptiness that is the true nature of all things.

All other possible states of mind are inevitably spoiled by destructive emotions. And wherever there are negative emotions, there will always be dissatisfaction and the feeling that things aren't the way they should be. Wealth, friends, fame—nothing helps. Why is it so hard to be happy and carefree? Why can't we just appreciate what we have? It is our anger, desire, and ignorance that mess it all up.

AN IMMEDIATE EFFECT

If we wish to be happy and of help to all others, then there's only one way forward—loving-kindness and insight into the emptiness that is the nature of things. Now, if we do take that path, will we be happy right away? And can we immediately guide others to happiness too? No, we cannot. But something *does* happen as soon as we embark on the path, because whenever we are loving, compassionate, and aware of emptiness, we simply cannot hurt anyone, either directly or indirectly.

But that's not all. Everything we do will automatically be helpful to others, both directly and indirectly. It's actually quite simple: helping others means giving them what they need. That may be something concrete such as money or food, or it may be something less tangible like safety and protection. Most valuable, however, is to pass on the insight that the Dharma has given us.

SADNESS, LOVE, AND INSIGHT

The Dharma is very clear about the causes of happiness and suffering. It also explains how to go beyond suffering, how to reach genuine and lasting happiness, and how to share that attainment with others. With a loving motivation and understanding of the way things are, we can explain to others the impermanence of all things. That's real sharing, because in that way we help others to see through their illusions.

The profound disillusionment that inevitably follows the recognition of impermanence is both natural and necessary. We shouldn't shy away from it, because love is born from that sorrow, and love yields insight into the way things really are.

These qualities and abilities are the source of perfect joy and happiness—for us and for all others. These are the qualities we should try to share and pass on.

THE LOVE OF A BODHISATTVA

In his classic account of the path of awakening, the Indian master Shantideva likens the love we feel for another person to the great love of a bodhisattva—a being on a path of compassionate awakening. When we love somebody, there is nothing we won't do to see that person happy. We are always ready to help, protect, and comfort. That's how love is. Love makes us patient. Love makes us persevere and endure.

We all know what it's like to love another person, and we can use this knowledge to understand what it means to be a bodhisattva. The big difference between the love we feel for another person and the love that a bodhisattva feels is that the bodhisattva's love isn't limited to certain individuals or to a select group of people. Instead, the bodhisattva harbors a deep-felt love for *all* beings and at the same time always endeavors to become wiser, warmer, and even more loving. The path of the bodhisattva is a journey toward wisdom and realization that is motivated by the wish to help others.

SIX ASPECTS OF BODHISATTVA TRAINING

What happens when we begin to think and act like bodhi-sattvas? What happens when our constant inspiration is the wish that all beings may enjoy happiness and the causes of happiness while remaining free from suffering and the causes of suffering? At that point, we begin to cultivate six extraordinary qualities: generosity, discipline, patience, enthusiasm, concentration, and insight. These are commonly referred to as the six perfections.

1. Generosity

Generosity is the practice of giving. It's the training in being generous with things, food, money, protection, and care. Generosity is born from love. We are already generous toward the ones we love, so generosity is a natural expression of love. But unlike ordinary people, a bodhisattva is generous toward *everybody*. And among all things we could possibly offer to others, the Dharma is the most precious.

2. Discipline

Discipline is the next quality, but what is discipline for a bodhisattva? It means living in accord with the wish not to harm anyone, and to do all that one can to be of benefit. That kind of discipline also springs from love. All excellent qualities blossom when a bodhisattva maintains this discipline in thought, word, and deed.

3. Patience

Love is patient, and the love of a bodhisattva endures all hardships, disappointments, pain, and hurt. Patience is the ability to accept adversity and not be discouraged. Patience opens our minds to the Dharma.

4. Enthusiasm

Enthusiasm is the joy of doing good deeds. A bodhisattva is deeply engaged in developing the qualities that are essential to the spiritual path—the wish to be free, loving-kindness, and insight. That process is fueled by great joy.

5. Concentration

Concentration refers to training the mind through meditation. Bodhisattvas have a balanced and composed mind. When the mind is calm and at ease, it also becomes agile and capable of wonderful achievements.

6. Insight

Insight arises from training in the first five qualities: generosity, discipline, patience, enthusiasm, and concentration. Insight is twofold: awareness of things as they appear and awareness of things as they really are. Insight dawns when the mind has achieved composure and agility by means of practice.

FOUR MEANS OF ATTRACTION

In their interactions with others, bodhisattvas also apply what are known as the *four means of attraction*. The first is to provide others with the things they wish for. The second is to speak in a way that is pleasant and delightful to listen to. The third is to teach in a way that is adjusted to the capacities and contexts of the audience. Finally, the fourth is to practice what one teaches. With those four means of attraction, others will naturally gather around us in a setting where the Dharma can flourish.

A GRADUAL PATH

The bodhisattva path is a gradual path. It begins with a wish to help others. When that wish is genuine, it will naturally affect the way we act. We need to be careful, however, not to overestimate ourselves and attempt to do things that we aren't ready for. It's important to allow the process to unfold naturally, and for our hearts to be in it all the way. If we bite off more than we can chew, nobody benefits.

Take the Buddhist ideal of infinite generosity, for instance. Here one is ready to give away even one's own body. That kind of generosity is not something that should be forced. Instead, our generosity must be natural and relaxed. As we begin to hold on to things less tightly and as we train in sharing with others, we will gradually become more adept at giving and more able to see clearly the benefits of generosity. Quietly but steadily, we become capable of increasingly greater deeds. This is true for all six aspects of the bodhisattva training. Our practice is not meant to break our backs or wear us down—it should be steady and natural.

SPROUTING SEEDS

The recognition of impermanence is the foundation for Buddhist practice. Spending time reflecting on the way everything conditioned is also impermanent is like plowing the fertile fields of our minds so the seeds that are naturally present in the soil can sprout. Love and compassion are like the rain and moisture that nourish the seeds. When the fields of our mind have been plowed with the realization of impermanence and watered with love and compassion, sprouts of insight grow. Over time, the sprouts evolve into three qualities: an acute awareness of impermanence, all-embracing love and compassion, and clear insight into the true nature of all things.

DASHED ILLUSIONS

We need to become aware of impermanence. The realization that everything disappears and that everything is unreliable is a devastating disappointment. As our dreams are shattered, we develop a nauseated sense of having had enough, and that revulsion in turn strengthens and nourishes our resolve to break free. Without that weariness, we lose focus. We become lazy and put off our training. Therefore, it is crucial that we realize the fundamental futility of our own existence.

No longer having to shoulder our illusions, we instead develop the ability to let go and set ourselves free. That happens because we understand that the world and all its inhabitants are doomed to disappear, and that, no matter what we may achieve, it won't last. The same goes for our emotions, our thoughts, and our ideas. Everything is temporary; everything is transient and impermanent. That realization comes with a deep sense of weariness that enables us to finally let go. What is there to covet and pursue? Suddenly we see the bigger picture—and let go.

There are many instructions, and much that we can be introduced to, but if we wish to come face-to-face with the way things really are, there's no way around acknowledging impermanence.

FROM LOVE TO WISDOM

The next step in our introduction to the way things really are is the recognition that negative emotions are the root of all negative actions and pain. Our own anger, desire, and ignorance create all our pain and misery. Conversely, love and compassion are the root of all that is good. With love and compassion, our actions are automatically wholesome and we feel good in both body and mind. When our minds are loving and compassionate, our negative emotions lose their footing, and when our destructive emotions fall away, our inherent wisdom has room to manifest. When we are told of this truth and personally acknowledge it, we have received a genuine introduction to the way things are.

BODHISATTVA MOTIVATION

Once we recognize impermanence and begin to view beings with love and compassion, the time has come to begin our bodhisattva training. As we have seen, bodhisattva training teaches us to be generous and develop discipline, to be patient and enthusiastic, and to train our consciousness so that it becomes more grounded and flexible. The goal is to reach insight into the way things really are while at the same time staying focused on the happiness and well-being of all others without exception. That is how we should train once we have understood that love and compassion are the root of all good and that destructive emotions are the root of all negativity. No matter our circumstances and no matter who might be in front of us, we are determined to do what is right, constructive, and most helpful to others. In short, we adapt our training to the situation at hand.

At the same time, we must take care not to develop any expectation of reward. Otherwise it's easy to end up thinking that we are special and that all the good deeds we do for others somehow ought to elicit a reward. But bodhisattvas are special precisely because they *don't* expect a reward or gratitude. In fact, bodhisattvas don't even consider their training to be a means for generating merit.

A bodhisattva's only motivation is the loving and compassionate attitude I just mentioned. Pain and suffering are caused by anger, desire, and ignorance, while all good things are due to love and compassion. As soon as we receive that instruction and take it to heart, we need to act on it. The way bodhisattvas act on that understanding is by training in the six perfections and the four means of attracting others.

WARNING SIGNS

Bodhisattva training is characterized by a total absence of competitiveness, envy, and conceit. So, if we find ourselves becoming envious or annoyed at those who are more generous, disciplined, or intelligent than we are, we can be certain that something is very wrong. It means that we have misunderstood something fundamental about our practice. Likewise, if we feel compelled to outdo our peers, or if we despise and feel superior to those beneath us, something has definitely gone wrong. In all such cases, we have missed the point of our practice!

THE TEACHINGS DEPEND ON THE LISTENER

People are different, and so the Buddha gave a great number of differing teachings. Various topics are emphasized, depending on the audience. Some people don't need to receive lengthy, detailed explanations in order to master their practice. They are naturally ready. For others, it's a bit more complicated, and still others require a lot of instruction. Because we are all different, the Buddha gave us different things to work with—different instructions that fit our individual capacities.

ELIMINATING DESIRE

Some people listen to the teachings of the Buddha and conclude that, since desire is the cause of destructive emotions and negative thought patterns, the main point is to eliminate personal wants and needs. Such people consider desire to be the biggest hindrance on the spiritual path, and so their practice focuses on eradicating desire. They choose a simple lifestyle and do not keep anything beyond the bare necessities. Based on such a modest and unassuming lifestyle, they train their minds to eliminate craving and fascination with impermanent phenomena. Instead, they commit themselves to cultivating insight into the true nature of things. Thereby they accomplish the realization that there is no individual self, or ego, and that is a liberating insight. That is one way to break free from conditioned existence.

THE BODHISATTVA PATH

Another set of instructions contains an insight that is sharper, involving practices that are more profound and transformative. This is known as the great vehicle, or the bodhisattva path. Here the goal is to realize the emptiness that is the true nature of all things and employ this realization for the benefit of all beings. Bodhisattvas train in arousing the mind of awakening. As they gradually master their training, they undergo a transformation—traditionally divided in five phases, known as "the five paths," and ten stages, called the "ten grounds". This process culminates in their attainment of the fully awakened state. In this way, bodhisattvas traverse the complete path to buddhahood. While others focus on overcoming desire, practitioners of the bodhisattva path primarily seek to overcome aggression and transform all destructive emotions into their positive counterparts.

THE VAJRA VEHICLE

These days, the teachings aimed at eliminating desire are practiced in countries such as Sri Lanka, Thailand, and Myanmar. In these countries, men and women become monks and nuns in order to train in contentment with only the most basic possessions while committed to the practice of meditation and insight. The various traditions that emphasize the bodhisattva path of compassionate engagement are to be found in countries such as Japan, Korea, and China. But there is also a third path, known as the vajra vehicle, or the tantric path, which has been practiced especially in Tibet. Thanks to the masters of the past, we still have access to the unique instructions and methods of the vajra vehicle. Those methods and instructions have brought great results, both in India where the tradition originated and later in Tibet where people kept the instructions alive and passed them on for the benefit of future generations. These instructions make the awakened state reachable quickly and with very little hardship.

THE FOUR OUTER PRELIMINARY PRACTICES

In the past, the masters of the vajra vehicle often began their training by reflecting on four topics that are expressed in four statements. We should also give careful and sincere thought to these four because they have the power to transform the way we think and the way we look at life.

1. Your current body is a precious tool.

2. Nothing lasts—everything changes and comes to an end.

3. All actions have consequences.

4. Life, death, and rebirth are characterized by suffering.

If we take these four statements to heart, we become fit for the practices that follow. That is why reflecting on these four points are known as the four *outer* preliminary practices.

However, in the vajra vehicle, it is crucial to also train in seeing everything as pure and perfect. Such pure perception is the foundation for all our practice in this vehicle, so we must always maintain the profound perspective of purity, even as we reflect on the four statements contained in the outer preliminaries.

RIGHT VIEW

Before we move to the inner preliminary practices, it would be appropriate to say a few words about insight. It is said that the insight one gains from the Buddha's teachings is insight into the way things really are. That insight we can also call *right view*. As we have already mentioned, right view is related to the understanding of dependent origination. When someone fully understands dependent origination, that person automatically adopts right view. It is said that phenomena are empty of any nature of their own because they arise in dependence on causes and conditions. Whenever we understand the meaning of that statement, not just intellectually but in our actual experience, we have arrived at right view.

Dependent origination is described as a chain of twelve links, the first of which is ignorance. With right view, we see how ignorance is the basis for the negative conditioning of our minds, and how it perpetuates the karmic actions that keep us tied in a vicious circle of cause and effect. Right view is the knowledge that cuts through and dissolves our fundamental ignorance. This knowledge leads to complete freedom from the painful cycle of birth, death, and rebirth—also known as samsara.

THE FOUR INNER PRELIMINARY PRACTICES

Contemplating the four outer preliminaries makes our minds stronger and more flexible. Our minds become like a fertile field cleared of rocks and weeds. The seeds we sow in such a field will sprout and turn into healthy crops. Once we have come that far, it is time to begin the four *inner* preliminary practices.

1. Refuge and the Mind of Awakening

The first of the four inner preliminary practices involves taking refuge and arousing the mind of awakening. Taking refuge in Buddha, Dharma, and Sangha and giving rise to the mind of awakening are combined with physical prostrations. The result is both a mental and a physical exercise that purifies us of all the negativity we have caused through the unwholesome use of our body—in this life as well as in all previous existences. The negativity is purified as we use our body to express our respect and devotion while mentally taking refuge in the Three Jewels and developing the mind of awakening. Refuge is the root of liberation. The mind of awakening is the root of omniscience. Their combination is the first of the four inner preliminary practices.

2. Meditation on Buddha Vajrasattva

The next spiritual exercise is the meditation on the buddha Vajrasattva. This practice also purifies, but this time the focus is particularly on all the negative things we have said. Here we aim to purify the negative effects of all the hurtful words we have ever spoken and all that we have said that has caused discord or misfortune, in this life as well as in all our past existences. All such misuse of our voice has had a negative impact on the way we are, and we continue to carry this negativity with us. Although caused by our voice, such unwholesome factors also manifest in our body and mind. To become free of that kind of negativity, we train in confessing our past negative actions, visualizing Vajrasattva, and perceiving the healing and purifying stream of nectar that flows from him as we recite his mantra.

3. Making Offerings

For practitioners of the vajra vehicle, the way to arrive at right view is by engaging in the third of the inner preliminary practices: the offering. This is a symbolic offering that involves outer, inner, and innermost levels of meaning. On the outer level, we offer all that is good, beautiful, and wholesome in the world. On the inner level, we offer our body and fortune. By making such outer and inner offerings, we are able to realize the way things truly are, beyond all concepts. That nonconceptual understanding is itself the innermost offering, and this is indeed the greatest offering possible.

The real reason we make offerings is to free ourselves from those misconceptions and wrong views that prevent the right view from dawning within us. As we make offerings to the buddhas and bodhisattvas, we purify the negativity that has built up from thinking and perceiving in a self-centered way that is out of touch with reality. In this way, by making offerings on three levels to the awakened buddhas, we purify our minds of all such negativity. That's how mental obscurations are removed according to the vajra vehicle.

4. Merging with the Guru

The last of the inner preliminaries is the practice of merging our minds with the wisdom mind of the guru. This practice, which is at the core of all training in the vajra vehicle, ensures great results, swiftly and easily. In this meditation, we receive the blessings of our main guru and all the other masters in the wisdom lineage. In this way, we connect with the awakened wisdom of the lineage; that is why this is such a powerful practice. By merging our minds with the guru, we become able to realize in our own experience, suddenly and directly, the purity of all phenomena—the crucial insight that lies at the heart of the teachings of the vajra vehicle.

In this practice, we first pray to our main guru as well as all lineage masters and all other awakened beings. We recall the precious qualities that these beings demonstrate with their body, speech, and mind, and we rejoice in those qualities. In particular, we rejoice in the power of their instructions—those instructions that enable us to care and provide for all beings, if only we take them to heart. We then supplicate these masters to bless us so that we may realize the nature of mind and lead all beings to liberation and awakening. Finally, we train by receiving empowerment from our main guru and merging our own mind with his or her wisdom mind, inseparably as one.

PURE PERCEPTION

The vajra vehicle has many methods, but they all hinge on whether we are able to perceive things as pure and perfect. If we have that ability, we can definitely gain a lot from practicing the vajra vehicle. But not many people are that fortunate. Our normal, ignorant consciousness is constantly engaged in unwholesome thinking, and we are always ready to act on our feelings of aversion, attachment, and ignorance. If we cannot relate to the instructions, our master, and our fellow practitioners with an understanding that everything is pure and perfect, then things can go very wrong. So, it is important to stay clear of doubt and wrong views. This, of course, is how we must relate to the teachings, our teacher, and our fellow practitioners, but it also applies to all other beings. Only then will our practice become flawless and pure. Ultimately, that is why we train in merging our minds with the wisdom mind of the guru.

SIGNS OF PROGRESS

The preliminary practices are both beneficial and practical. We should train in them with an open and sincere mind. We should not rush through the practices, but we must also not drag them out indefinitely. When we begin these practices, we will notice that our minds begin to change. The way we react is different from before; clarity, warmth, and strength blossom from within. We are more balanced and flexible, and our impulses and emotions have less of a grip on us. Gradually, we become more caring, devoted, and intelligent. Those are the surest signs that the preliminary practices are working as intended. There are also other signs that our training is effective, but those are secondary. Such signs can appear in dreams, for example.

EMPOWERMENT

When we have completed both the inner and outer preliminary practices, we have truly stepped onto the path of the vajra vehicle. Then it becomes time to receive the ripening empowerments and the liberating instructions. That is how wisdom is transmitted in the vajra vehicle. We say that the mind is matured through empowerment and liberated through instruction.

The ripening empowerments introduce us to the way things really are. As we have talked about before, the words *introduction* and *pointing out* should be understood in that way—bringing us face-to-face with the way things really are. In the vajra vehicle, such an introduction typically takes place through a ritual of four empowerments conferred by a qualified master to a student. Each empowerment introduces a particular insight. These four insights can be described as follows:

All sights are visible emptiness.

All sounds are audible emptiness.

All sensations are blissful emptiness.

All concepts are thought-free wakefulness.

The first two—showing that whatever we see and hear is indivisible from emptiness—are also explained in the philosophy of the great vehicle. The difference is that the great vehicle conveys these points through philosophical reflection, whereas in the vajra vehicle these insights are actual experiences transmitted by means of a ritual.

The third empowerment reveals that all sensations are blissful emptiness. Here the subtle channels, energies, and essences within the body are used to facilitate the realization that all sensations—whether pleasant, unpleasant, or neutral—are in fact nothing but great bliss. Unlike the first two empowerments, this process is unique to the vajra vehicle. So is the fourth empowerment, the revelation that the true nature of thoughts is primordial thought-free wakefulness. The essence of thought is thought-free wakefulness. When this is pointed out to us, we can directly recognize that the nature of thoughts is wisdom.

In the vajra vehicle, there are many practices and approaches. But the perspective of the fourth and final empowerment is the culmination of them all. Here we are brought face-to-face with the true nature of thoughts—we experience the nature of thoughts as thought-free wakefulness. It is crucial, however, for our experience to be authentic; otherwise it cannot lead to authentic realization. If we intellectualize the fourth empowerment and misunderstand its significance, then the path is closed off. If we believe that we have had an experience of the way things are, and yet that is not the case, then the path is blocked, because everything we do subsequently will unfold based on a false premise.

MISUNDERSTANDING EMPTINESS

We need to be clear about the right view. The view is the basis for our training. It is our understanding of the view that determines whether our practice is authentic. If we develop wrong view, there will be errors across the board. Indeed, the nature of misunderstanding is to incorrectly think that one has understood. For instance, in the context of Buddhist philosophy, this might occur if we feel that our understanding of emptiness is perfect even though we only have an intellectual understanding of emptiness, which is a far cry from the profundity of actual, experiential insight. If that misunderstanding is left unchecked, our practice can degenerate into a habit of just ruminating on a set of choice concepts—and so we get stuck spiritually. To gain a real understanding of emptiness, we must receive instructions directly from a realized master who has an actual experience of emptiness him- or herself.

MISUNDERSTANDING THE NATURE OF MIND

Just as we can be wrong about emptiness, we can also be mistaken about the nature of mind. For example, we might think that we know how to sustain the recognition of the nature of mind, while in fact we don't. Perhaps we think that it's just a matter of being mindful of our thoughts as they come and go. All we do then is sit and watch our thoughts. We try to monitor every little impulse and perception. Unfortunately, that has nothing whatsoever to do with recognizing the nature of mind.

MISUNDERSTANDING WAKEFULNESS

The same goes for the mind's original wakefulness. Realizing primordial wakefulness is a matter of recognizing thought-free wakefulness. When we hear that, we might get the impression that we just have to make sure not to have any thoughts. But just having no thoughts is surely not the same as actualizing thought-free wakefulness. Thought-free wakefulness is bright, sharp, vivid, and direct. It has to unfold like that, if we want the recognition of thought-free wakefulness to be our practice. In other words, it is crucial that we see things as they are. Otherwise our misunderstanding can quickly take us down a dead end.

THE SUPREME GUIDE

The preliminary practices save us from dead ends. That is also the reason we seek guidance in Buddhist teachings—that is why the words of the Buddha have been passed on from generation to generation and why we study the classical commentaries and treatises to this day. The oral instructions serve the same purpose, but it's crucial to receive them from someone who already embodies the insight and experience that the instructions are meant to transmit. In other words, our teacher has to be someone who has realized the true nature of reality—someone we can trust because he or she speaks from experience. That kind of teacher can faultlessly communicate the instructions to us and ensure that we don't misunderstand them. That is why it's so important to meet a qualified guide and keep contact with him or her until it's all perfectly clear to us.

A SPECIAL PATH

All Buddhist traditions focus on arriving at the right view. Still, these days it seems that many people are particularly interested in the instructions of the vajra vehicle. That's undoubtedly because the vajra vehicle doesn't require us to give up the things we enjoy in life. Indeed, in the vajra vehicle such things are considered the very path of awakening. The five destructive emotions—delusion, desire, anger, pride, and envy are seen as the path to awakening in a single lifetime, and samsara is recognized as the awakened state itself.

A CALM MIND

If we want the five destructive emotions to be our path to awakening in a single lifetime, then we need the right view and our practice must be in accord with the fundamental purity of all things. Everything stands and falls with the introduction to the nature of mind and our recognition of the right view. To achieve the right view, there are a number of things we can do.

For instance, one special technique prepares us for the right view by allowing our minds to relax and quiet down. It is easier to recognize the right view when the mind is calm. At the same time, we must understand that this technique is merely a means and not an end in itself. *Calm mind is not the same as liberation.* But unless our minds are calm, our ability to realize the way things are cannot develop. That's why it is sometimes said that insight requires a calm mind.

If you take a glass of murky water and keep stirring it, the water will never become clear. But if you stop stirring, the impurities will slowly sink to the bottom until finally the water is perfectly clear. Our mind is the same way. When we stop feeding our thoughts and let the mind settle, it clears up all by itself.

UNCONTRIVED NATURALNESS

There are many kinds of mental calm, but in the vajra vehicle we find a kind that is particularly useful. It is called *uncontrived naturalness*. That type of meditation is very simple. All we need to do is let the mind be, exactly as it is:

> *Produce nothing, suppress nothing. Just let your mind be, exactly as it is, right now, in this very moment, completely free from hopes or expectations.*

It sounds easy and straightforward—and it *is* easy. However, because the habit of doing and acting is so ingrained in our being, it can actually be very difficult not to do anything at all. So we need to be aware and continuously remind ourselves that there isn't anything to do. When we remember to simply let the mind be, just as it is, then the mind assumes a natural poise. That kind of mental calm is the best possible calmness. From there, true insight can begin to unfold.

TECHNIQUE VERSUS REALIZATION

When the mind is at rest, there is space for true wisdom to unfold. It is therefore crucial for us to know how to calm the mind. To achieve a calm mind, there is no better method than simply resting naturally in the present moment. But remember: this is just a method, not a goal in itself! Letting the mind rest in uncontrived naturalness is not the same as having recognized the nature of mind. It is the gateway to realization, wisdom, and insight, *but not identical with realization.* It is so important to understand that difference. Resting the mind in uncontrived naturalness is a technique that facilitates the birth of wisdom. When mind is allowed to rest naturally, just as it is, then recognizing the nature of mind is not difficult at all.

MANY METHODS, ONE PURPOSE

There are many things we can do to rest in uncontrived naturalness and recognize the nature of mind. Many practices help clear the obscurations in our minds and bring the right conditions together. All the many techniques, practices, studies, reflections, contemplations, and meditations share a single goal—facilitating our recognition of the nature of mind. That's also why we pray to the awakened masters and ask them for blessings and help. This is why we train in mingling our minds indivisibly with their awakened mind. That training has one purpose—to enable our recognition of the nature of mind.

SOLITUDE

If you wish to realize the nature of mind, it is helpful to spend time in a peaceful, quiet place where there are no distractions. Find a remote place, far from worldly affairs, where you can focus on the Dharma. That is the best place to be. There you can put aside the worries and concerns of everyday life and instead spend time on what truly matters. Masters of the past did this, and so should we. As beginners, we will find progress close to impossible unless we set aside special periods for our practice. We need to spend time in retreat. That's how our practice can pick up speed and gain impetus. Tibetan tradition recommends that we set aside three years for practice in retreat. If that's not possible, then try with a couple of months of retreat every year. Two or three weeks should be the minimum, but any amount of retreat will of course be beneficial.

OUR TIME, OUR CHOICE

If we don't set aside time for practice, then we must be honest with ourselves and admit that it's going to be very difficult to take advantage of the extraordinary opportunity we have right now in this life. At the moment we are alive, but our life is running out whether we want it or not. With every passing day, our life is one day shorter. No matter how we decide to spend our life, it will soon be all over.

Maybe you're busy and have many commitments. Perhaps you feel you have lots of expectations to live up to. But is the rest of your life really fully booked already? Don't you get any say as to how you spend your time? Think about it. Is there really no free time during the day? Of course there is. In fact, we all have a great deal of influence on the way our life is structured. So why not exercise your influence now and set aside time for practice? If you schedule time in a place that is conducive for practice and has few distractions, you will be able to go far.

NOT A MATTER OF WATCHING

Once we are in a place where we can focus wholeheartedly on practice, the mind can settle and calm down. Then, when the mind is at ease, it can develop insight into its own nature. As we allow our body, our voice, and our mind to rest in naturalness, we should remind ourselves: *The view is not a matter of watching, so give up the act of looking!*

What happens when we take such an instruction to heart? As the mind rests in uncontrived naturalness, we remind ourselves that the right view cannot be produced or developed. Then, what else can we do besides dropping all reference points, including the very idea of getting the view right? When all efforts and reference points are dropped completely, the basic nature of the mind is laid bare and the realization of the right view dawns by itself.

WE KNOW VERY WELL

We know very well that unless we set aside time to practice, we'll never get around to it. Knowing something to be absolutely crucial and yet ignoring it isn't just pointless—it's absurd. It's like a person dying of thirst on the shore of a great lake. That is a good analogy to keep in mind.

THE GRIP OF CONSCIOUSNESS

Right view is the gateway to liberation. Our ignorant mind that spins in samsara is produced by our thoughts. Our thoughts are the basis for the negative emotions that drive our delusion and cause pain and misery for everyone. "Thinking" is our grasping mind. Thinking is our mind when it locks on to something and is unable to let go. This is the root of all our problems: the grasping mind that cannot let go.

This is a very important point. If our thoughts are causing the problem—if in fact they *are* the problem—then working with our thoughts is not a viable solution. It doesn't matter how skilled we may be at focusing and directing our attention, because it's exactly there—in the grip of consciousness—that the trouble starts.

THOUGHT-FREE WAKEFULNESS

Only a complete absence of thoughts can free us. We must achieve a state of wakefulness that is perfectly clear and thought-free. For that, no sort of meditation training is going to be useful because there is nothing to keep in mind, nothing to focus on, and nowhere to direct our attention. So give up the idea of meditation and you will no longer be distracted.

Thought-free wakefulness dissolves the grip of our ignorant, dualistic mind. Thought-free wakefulness blows up the grammar of ordinary consciousness and goes beyond subject, object, and action. Thought-free wakefulness cannot be grasped by thought. It is—quite literally—*unthinkable*. Still, we can train our consciousness to recognize it. Among the many techniques we can use, letting our mind rest in uncontrived naturalness is one of the best.

OUR TRUE NATURE

I have mentioned this many times already; we must understand that all conditioned things are impermanent and thereby see through all the deceptions that usually fool us. When we do that, it's hard not to feel revulsion toward the whole situation. With revulsion and disenchantment, the wish for freedom is kindled—a fervent longing for freedom that inspires and fuels all we do. Impermanence hurts . . . but the reason we contemplate death and destruction is not that we love to feel down. We do it because it gives us the courage and strength to look at the world with love and compassion. Love and compassion heal the mind. When we look at the world with loving eyes, all harmful thoughts and emotions vanish naturally.

In this way, love and compassion enhance our understanding and training. The instructions tell us to release the hold of our dualistic mind. In the very moment conceptual mind releases its grip, we acknowledge the wakefulness that is the true nature of all beings. That's how we all truly are. We get this as a direct experience whenever the conceptual mind is suspended and our usual dualistic perception has collapsed.

Our meditation is uncontrived naturalness. Remember the example of the murky water—if you leave the water alone, it clears on its own. The same goes for the mind. If we don't keep consciousness occupied, it settles—and the nature of mind reveals itself.

WIDE OPEN LIKE THE SKY

How do we become true practitioners of the vajra vehicle? It all depends on the mind and consciousness. Our minds have to transform into the mind of a practitioner—wide open and utterly beyond the tiny cage of thinking. Our minds must become boundless and unimpeded, like the wide-open sky. That's how to practice. Consciousness has released its grip and there's no longer anything to hold on to or anyone holding on. That's the perfect practice. All that remains is wisdom—unadulterated, pure wakefulness. *That* is insight into the nature of reality— original pure wakefulness. This insight differs from all other types of understanding and recognition, because right there, in that very moment, reality is seen and recognized, just as it is. It is the true nature of all beings. It is the awakening of all buddhas.

BEYOND HOPE AND FEAR

When the grip of the conceptual mind is undone, the original state appears and all the wonderful qualities that we have heard so much about are given the space to unfold. The buddhas' infinite love and compassion, the wisdom that sees everything while realizing the true nature of all—such qualities manifest from thought-free wakefulness. There is no longer anything to hope for. There is no longer anything to fear. We have broken free of all the different chains of the conceptual mind. The Tibetan master Gotsangpa once said:

> The mind of an ordinary person
> Is never anything but awakened wisdom.
> If you recognize that even without having to be
>   shown by a master,
> Then there you go!

THE ESSENCE OF THE BUDDHIST TEACHING

We need to practice the heart of the teachings. That is what I try to do myself, and although I'm not always successful, I do my best. Here are three instructions that summarize the essence of the Buddha's teachings:

Understanding that this world is impermanent and your time is short, lessen attachment and learn to let go.

Regard all beings as your own parents and train tirelessly in being generous, disciplined, patient, enthusiastic, concentrated, and wise.

The nature of your mind is perfect awakening—understand, experience, and realize that.

There is also a fourth instruction, which is found only in the vajra vehicle. It tells us to seek out a person who can point out to us the nature of mind—a guru with experience and integrity. Such a person can bring us face-to-face with the nature of mind, and when *that* happens, all obstacles fall away. Knowing such a person is a source of incredible power and strength. The fourth and final instruction is therefore:

Regard your master as a buddha and let your minds merge indivisibly.

ABOUT THE AUTHOR

Chokyi Nyima Rinpoche is a world-renowned Buddhist teacher and meditation master. Born in Tibet in 1951, he is the firstborn son of his mother Kunsang Dechen, a devoted Buddhist practitioner, and his father Tulku Urgyen Rinpoche, an accomplished master of Buddhist meditation. As a young child, he was recognized as the seventh incarnation of the Tibetan meditation master Gar Drubchen and installed as the head lama of Drong Monastery in the Nakchukha region, north of the capital city Lhasa.

In 1959, following the occupation of Tibet, Rinpoche fled with his family to India and Nepal, where he spent his youth studying under some of Tibetan Buddhism's most illustrious masters, including the Sixteenth Karmapa, Dilgo Khyentse Rinpoche, and Tulku Urgyen Rinpoche. In 1976 he was enthroned as the abbot of Ka-Nying Shedrub Ling Monastery in Kathmandu, which still today remains the heart of his ever-growing activity. Today, more than 500 monks and nuns are under his care in this and other monasteries in Nepal. Drong Monastery, which was completely destroyed during the Cultural Revolution, has recently been rebuilt and is again home to a monastic community.

Chokyi Nyima Rinpoche is the founder and spiritual head of numerous centers for Buddhist study and meditation in Asia, Europe, and North America. In Nepal, he runs Rangjung Yeshe Institute, an international center of learning where students can obtain BA, MA, and PhD degrees in Buddhist Studies. For those who wish to study and practice from home, Rinpoche also offers an online meditation program that covers the entire Buddhist path. At home in Nepal, he is deeply involved in social work through his local charity organization Shenpen.

To read more about Chokyi Nyima Rinpoche and his activities, visit www.shedrub.org.